PENGUIN BOOKS
THE LOST GOON SHOWS

Spike Milligan was born in Ahmednagar in India in 1918. He received his first education in a tent in the Hyderabad Sindh desert and graduated from there, through a series of Roman Catholic schools in India and England, to the Lewisham Polytechnic. Always something of a playboy, he then plunged into the world of Show Business, seduced by his first stage appearance, at the age of eight, in the nativity play of his Poona convent school. He began his career as a band musician but has since become famous as a humorous script writer and actor in both films and broadcasting. He was one of the main figures in and behind the infamous Goon Show. Among the films he has appeared in are *Suspect*, *Invasion*, *Postman's Knock* and *Milligan at Large*.

Spike Milligan's published work includes *The Little Potboiler*, *Silly Verse for Kids*, *Dustbin of Milligan*, *A Book of Bits*, *The Bed-sitting Room* (a play), *The Bald Twit Lion*, *A Book of Milliganimals*, *Puckoon*, *Small Dreams of a Scorpion*, *Transports of Delight*, *The Milligan Book of Records*, *Games, Cartoons and Commercials*, *Dip the Puppy*, *William McGonagall: The Truth at Last* (with Jack Hobbs), *The Spike Milligan Letters* and *More Spike Milligan Letters*, both edited by Norma Farnes, *Open Heart University*, *The Q Annual*, *Unspun Socks from a Chicken's Laundry*, *The 101 Best and Only Limericks of Spike Milligan*, *There's a Lot of It About*, *The Melting Pot*, *Further Transports of Delight* and *The Looney: An Irish Fantasy*. His incomparable six volumes of war memoirs are *Adolf Hitler: My Part in His Downfall*, *'Rommel?' 'Gunner Who?'*, *Monty: His Part in My Victory*, *Mussolini: His Part in My Downfall*, *Where Have All the Bullets Gone?* and *Goodbye Soldier*. To celebrate his seventieth birthday Penguin have published a special edition of his first novel, *Puckoon*.

The LOST GOON SHOWS

SPIKE MILLIGAN

Penguin Books

Goon Show admirers might like to know of:

The Goon Show Preservation Society
24 Oakland Avenue
Hartlepool
Cleveland TS25 5LD
(Secretary: Christopher Smith)

PENGUIN BOOKS

Published by the Penguin Group
27 Wrights Lane, London W8 5TZ, England
Viking Penguin Inc., 40 West 23rd Street, New York, New York 10010, USA
Penguin Books Australia Ltd, Ringwood, Victoria, Australia
Penguin Books Canada Ltd, 2801 John Street, Markham, Ontario, Canada L3R 1B4
Penguin Books (NZ) Ltd, 182–190 Wairau Road, Auckland 10, New Zealand

Penguin Books Ltd, Registered Offices: Harmondsworth, Middlesex, England

First published by Robson Books 1987
Published in Penguin Books 1988

Copyright © Spike Milligan, 1987
All rights reserved

Designed by Harold King

Drawings (mostly) by Spike Milligan

Thanks are owed to Mrs Larry Stephens for permission
to include 'Operation Christmas Duff'

Made and printed in Great Britain by
Richard Clay Ltd, Bungay, Suffolk

CONTENTS

Early days. The original quartet: Michael Bentine, Spike Milligan, Peter Sellers, Harry Secombe

BBC

INTRODUCTION

This, I presume, will be the last time some Goon Shows will go into print.

It's nigh on 35 years since that distant first show which, though full of enthusiasm, was pretty amateurish and really not very funny – however, we hung on in there and learned as we went along.

To my astonishment, I have discovered that there are Goon Show Preservation Societies all over Britain, Australia and America, and that the Goon Show is still being heard twice weekly in Australia, as it is in America. This makes it the longest-running comedy show ever, and I've written to the *Guinness Book of Records* informing them. They ignore my letters, so I've stopped drinking Guinness.

After all these years, these 'lost' Goon Shows didn't seem that funny to me and I've rewritten here and there to jolly them up a little. I hope they jolly you up a little.

p.s. Since writing this, I have discovered an unfinished Goon Show – for some reason never completed and therefore never performed. Alas, with Sellers gone, it never can be. But though it's too late, it's not too late to include it in this little volume.

Spike Milligan

SPIKE MILLIGAN, 1987

Spike Milligan with Larry Stephens, his collaborator on
'Operation Christmas Duff'

OPERATION CHRISTMAS DUFF

The Goon Show: Special Overseas Edition
Recorded 9th December 1956
First Transmission 24th December, 1956 (General Overseas Service only)
Second Transmission Christmas Day, 1986 (Radio 4)

Cast (main characters)

Spike Milligan
>   Statisticker
>   Sparks
>   Seaman
>   Batman
>   Captain Berk
>   Eccles
>   Moriarty

Peter Sellers
>   Minister of Military-type Foods
>   Dimbleby
>   Major Bloodnok
>   Churchill
>   Bluebottle
>   Grytpype

Harry Secombe
>   Admiral Seagoon
>   Captain Thing

With The Ray Ellington Quartet, Max Geldray, and the
Orchestra conducted by Wally Stott.
Script by Spike Milligan and Larry Stephens.
Announcer Wallace Greenslade.
Producer Pat Dixon.

● ● ● ● ● ● ● ● ● ● ● ● ● ●

Entrusted with the task of driving a giant Christmas pudding to the Forces Overseas (minus one slice destined for the Trans-Antarctic Expedition), Eccles and Bluebottle run into trouble in the shape of two starving ne'er-do-wells, Moriarty and Grytpype. Meanwhile, in the icy arctic wastes, their strength ebbing away, Admiral Seagoon and Major Bloodnok are on the horns of a classic dilemma: whether to have their pudding, or eat it. The choice is agonizing . . .

WALLACE This programme is specially dedicated to Her Majesty's Forces Overseas and to the Trans-Antarctic Expedition, the Falkland Islands Dependency Survey Teams, the Royal Society Expedition at Halle Bay, and Mrs Rita Body. Greetings from the Goons.

ECCLES Hallo.

ORCHESTRA *Regal fanfare*

PETER This is the story of a great endeavour.

ECCLES Is it?

PETER A story of land, sea and air. And in some cases, both. The date: the 23rd November 1956. Christmas was coming. The geese were getting fat. Someone spent a penny in an old man's hat. But one problem lay heavily on Parliament's conscience.

FX	*(fade in) Crowd of Greeks talking*
MINISTER	Gentlemen – as Minister of Military-type Foods, I must say the picture regarding Christmas puddings for the forces overseas looks pretty black.
MP	Why don't we send them black puddings?
ORCHESTRA	*Corny chord*
PETER	Thank you, Sir Hartley Shawcross KC. And now, a few statistics from our resident statisticker.
ORCHESTRA	*Lively introductory-type music*
STATISTICKER	I say, I say, I say. I say, gentlemen, owing to the shortage of civilian compressors, they cannot supply sufficient Xmas-type duff for our forces overseas.
OLD MAN	What about the Naafi?
FIRST VOICE	Naafi – what is Naafi?
SECOND VOICE	An organization working for the downfall of the British Army.
STATISTICKER	Gentlemen, gentlemen, I have a solution. I just took it off a bicycle tyre. Now, listen to me, please. Why don't the services all combine in the building of a giant Services Christmas pudding?
FX	*Crowd – applause, cheers, fade in singing of 'Land of Hope and Glory'*
PETER	The motion was adopted and passed. But meanwhile, at the Admiralty –
FX	*Bosun's whistle*

SPARKS   Pardon me, sir RN.

SEAGOON   What is it?

SPARKS   I am sorry to interrupt you at squash, sir.

SEAGOON   It's all right, I'll drink it later.

SPARKS   This morse signal's just arrived from Magadan Trans-Antarctic Expedition, sir.

SEAGOON   What does it say?

SPARKS   I don't know, it's all little dots and dashes.

SEAGOON   Play it on the gramophone.

SPARKS   Right. (*Beeping sound*) Is it code?

Neddie Seagoon

SEAGOON   Yes – stoke up the fire. (*Morse code bleeping continues*) Of course! It's in Morse – I speak it fluently. It's We-Want-a-Christmas-Pudding-for-Christmas-by-the-boys-of-the-Trans-Antarctic-Expedition with-Taffy-Williams-at-the-Mighty-Morse-Keys. Gad, it means those lads out there in all that sand and snow are pudding-less!

SPARKS   I fear so, sir.

SEAGOON   It's not British, I tell you, it's not British.

SPARKS   No, sir – most Christmas puddings are made-in-Japan pluddings.

SEAGOON   Wait! I have it!

SPARKS   Yes, I can see you've got it, sir.

SEAGOON   We will have to ask the service chiefs to increase the size of the giant Service Christmas pudding to allow for an extra slice for the Antarctic base.

SPARKS   Yes, sir. E'en now they're mixing it at Chatham. I'll drive you there.

FX   *Whip cracks. Two men running away*

GRAMS   *'Claire de Lune'*

WALLACE   We included that brief excerpt from 'Claire de Lune' for people who speak French. Now, over to Richard Dimbleby.

FX   *Machinery – very complicated, spurts, plops etc*

● ● ● ● ● ● ● ● ● ● ● ● ● ●

DIMBLEBY The sound you are now hearing is the combined Services Christmas pudding in the making. I am standing by the great dry dock at Chatham in which the Christmas pudding is being mixed. Standing next to me, two feet lower down is Admiral Seagoon.

FX *Bosun's whistle*

SEAGOON Ah, that's better! Well, we've had a good day for pudding. Number three flotilla torpedo boats have been going backwards and forwards churning up the mixture. The cruiser Ajax has been following in their wake, dropping depth charges to bring the raisins to the surface.

DIMBLEBY The finest traditions of the silent service being maintained.

FX *Bosun's whistle*

SEAGOON Ah, that's better! Yes, yes, we try to keep the men happy when they're off duty by giving them little tasks like this.

DIMBLEBY We could do with more of that spirit.

SEAMAN (*uncouth*) You could both do with a big clout up the back of your big fat steaming nuts.

SEAGOON Our nuts are not steaming – arrest that stoker.

DIMBLEBY How do you test the density of this great Service pudding?

SEAGOON We sent a diver down half an hour ago. It was silly, really.

BBC

DIMBLEBY Why?

SEAGOON He hasn't got a diving suit on, ha ha – he he!

DIMBLEBY (*very earnest*) The best tradition of the Navy cake!

FX *Aeroplane*

DIMBLEBY And now the great dockyard is being cleared, as the fairy gannets of 824 Squadron swoop low over the pudding. Their bomb bays are open, and yes, down comes the candied peel, ginger and sultanas.

● ● ● ● ● ● ● ● ● ● ● ● ●

FX *Bomb descending, and crash*

DIMBLEBY A direct hit on the great Christmas pudding mixture! A grand day for the Royal Air Force and Miss Muriel Body.

SEAMAN Pardon me, sir, oil tankers standing by to take on the pudding!

SEAGOON Right – drop the suction pumps into the mixture and suck it!

SEAMAN (*off*) Aye aye, sir.

FX *Suction pump, slurping noises*

DIMBLEBY And so the great pudding mixture is siphoned out of the dry dock and into the all-British oil tanker, *Aristotle Onassis,* which is registered as a bakery in Rangoon.

SEAGOON Yes, it'll be transported overland to an empty gasometer near Salisbury Plain. From then the pudding is under Army command. Unfortunately.

DIMBLEBY Thank you, Admiral Seagoon. Now over to Max Geldray for some rum and baccy.

MAX AND ORCHESTRA Music

WALLACE Operation Christmas Duff, Part Two.

FX	*Bugle call all wrong*
BLOODNOK	Oh, it's – er – what is it? Of course, it's reveille. And first thing in the morning, too. What a shock. Quick, batman – brandy – brandy!
BATMAN	Have you got a weak heart?
BLOODNOK	No, a weak will.
BATMAN	Oh! So have I, sir. (*Drinking*)
BLOODNOK	Put that bottle down!
BATMAN	I'm trying to, sir.
BLOODNOK	Give me that. (*Drinking*)
FX	*Tap dripping*
BATMAN	You're leaking, sir.
CAPTAIN THING	Major! 0600 hours, sir, transporter arrived with converted gasometer with 600 tons of Christmas pudding ready for cooking, sir!
BLOODNOK	Oh, Captain Thing! What's its map reference?
CAPTAIN THING	7981 – Salisbury Plain, sir!
BLOODNOK	Where's that?
CAPTAIN THING	You're standing on it, sir!
BLOODNOK	I'm sorry, I hope I haven't dirtied it.

● ● ● ● ● ● ● ● ● ● ● ● ● ●

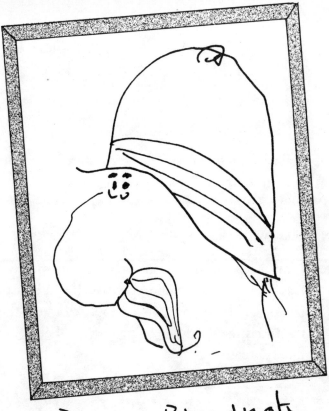

Dennis Bloodnok

CAPTAIN THING   It's all right, sir! We have it blanco'd every other day.

      FX   *Knocks at door*

CAPTAIN THING   Knocks on door, sir!

BLOODNOK   Come in! – Two! – Three!

      FX   *Navy whistle*

SEAGOON   Ah, that's better!

BLOODNOK   Oh, it's an Admiral. What are you doing so far on military land?

SEAGOON   I ran aground, sir. I was sent along to report on the cooking.

BLOODNOK   Follow me. (*Footsteps*) The Derbyshire Yeomanry have laid on fourteen flame-throwing tanks.

FX   *Bugle — 'Come to the cook-house door'. Mad stampede of soldiers*

SEAGOON   I say, what call is that?

BLOODNOK   Cook-house! Number one on our hit parade, you know. Has been for three hundred years. If you'll just come into this observation post you'll be able to watch the whole of the Christmas pudding being cooked. Let's go over to the radar screen.

FX   *Electronic noises. Flame-throwers. Tanks*

WALLACE   Hello, listeners. The sound you're hearing are the tanks which are bringing their flame-throwers to bear, as they cook the giant Christmas pudding in its gasometer.

CAPTAIN BERK   At dawn this morning, number forty-five commando went in under cover of daylight, and brought back samples for testing by the Army Catering Corps.

WALLACE   What was it like?

CAPTAIN BERK   Pretty good.

BLOODNOK   Ah, Captain Berk.

CAPTAIN BERK   Two, three, four, Sah!

BLOODNOK   Field Intelligence reports that the pudding is done.

CAPTAIN BERK   Absolutely first class. I should wait till things have cooled down a bit, then send in the Sappers to blast open the gasometer with Bangalore torpedoes.

WALLACE   Excuse me, Major, I'm from the BBC.

BLOODNOK   I'm sorry, I don't have any money on me.

FX   *Distant atom bomb*

BLOODNOK   Oh, there she goes! You see that? Split the gasometer completely in two. Well done, Sappers.

WALLACE   Indeed, listeners. Right in two, revealing a great, steaming, Services Christmas pudding.

FX   *Gunfire*

WALLACE   And there you hear the 74th Medium Regiment RA firing over open sights smack into the pudding itself. Tell me, Major, what are they firing?

BLOODNOK   Threepenny bits.

CAPTAIN BERK   Excuse me, sir, the infantry CO is on the walkie-talkie.

BLOODNOK   Hello? Sunray here.

SEAGULL   Seagull speaking – sit. rep., sir. B Company 2nd Force have reached the summit of the Christmas pudding.

BLOODNOK   Right, consolidate! Roger and out. Gentlemen, the Army's task in this matter is completed. It is now under RAF command. Unfortunately.

GRAMS   '*Dam Busters March*'

HARRY   That night, an excited House was given the news.

FX   *Crowd noise – heavy mutterings – occasional chicken*

CHURCHILL   Honourable members, I have this moment received good news. At 1700 hours British troops gained the summit of the combined Services Christmas pudding and there planted the British holly.

FX   *Applause and cheers*

CHURCHILL   One hour later, the Canberras of Bomber Command dropped delayed custard bombs, followed by brandy torpedoes – then napalm to set it alight.

FX   *Cheers – all sing 'Land of Hope and Glory'*

WALLACE   Late that night, Service chiefs were given their instructions at the War Office.

FX   *Bar room noises – honky tonk piano, drunken singing, 'Oh Danny Boy' etc*

SEAGOON   Gentlemen, please, please. If the Chief of the Imperial General Staff will lay off the piano! Thank you. I have here sealed orders containing four tickets for the

● ● ● ● ● ● ● ● ● ● ● ● ●

Windmill, and this message: 'The pudding will be divided as follows: One slice to be cut and filled with anti-freeze for immediate transport to the Trans-Antarctic expedition. The remainder of the giant Christmas pudding will be fitted with wheels, a diesel engine, and driven to the Middle East depots for distribution. Signed, Field Marshal Montgoonery.'

GRAMS *Eastern music*

FX *Sand storm. Heavy vehicle struggling over terrain*

BLUEBOTTLE Have you ever driven a Christmas pudding before?
ECCLES No, I never driven **anything** before.

BLUEBOTTLE Then how did you get the job?

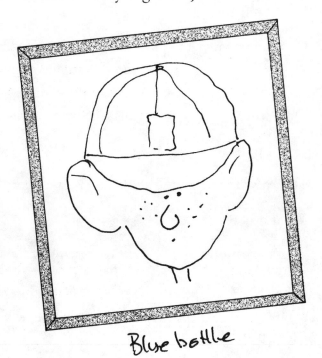

Blue bottle

Eccles

ECCLES   The Sergeant said, one pace forward anyone who can play the piano.

BLUEBOTTLE   Oh. Can you play the piano then?

ECCLES   No.

BLUEBOTTLE   Then why are you driving this Christmas pudding?

ECCLES   I want to learn to play the piano.

BLUEBOTTLE   Then it's **true** what the recruiting posters say.

ECCLES   What do they say?

BLUEBOTTLE   'You're **somebody** in the modern army of today'.

ECCLES   Oh. And what are you?

BLUEBOTTLE   I'm somebody in the modern army of today.

ECCLES   Oh. I wondered who you were. How did you join?

BLUEBOTTLE   I was in the street writing something on the wall. I was only writing my name.

ECCLES   Wouldn't they know who done it then?

BLUEBOTTLE   No, I didn't sign it. Then up comes a naughty hairy man wearing a soldier set, and he said 'Little Finchley lad, you don't want to write your name in little silly chalk. You want to write your name in ink.' And then I said 'Where?' And he said 'On this nice military dotted line.' So I signed it. Then they said 'Can you play the piano?' and I said 'Yes.' And here I am.

ECCLES   Give us a tune.

BLUEBOTTLE   What would you like?

ECCLES   My ticket.

BLUEBOTTLE   How does it go?

ECCLES   It goes (*sings*): Doctor, my dear military doctor, you gotta believe me, I got a bad back in the front. I'm not fit for active service, I gotta bone in my leg. And when I close my eyes I can't see. When I lie down it hurts me to lie sideways (*he fades away enumerating diseases*).

QUARTET   *'Old Man River'*

GRYTPYPE   Moriarty –

MORIARTY (*toothless*) What? Can't you see I'm busy licking a jam spoon?

GRYTPYPE Tell us who we are.

Grytpype-
Thynne

MORIARTY This **us** is Moriarty, and this us is Grytpype.

GRYTPYPE What's that coming round the mountain pass in Cyrenaica?

MORIARTY Hand me my telescopic wig, I'll just trim the fringe.

FX . *Scissors*

MORIARTY Ah yes. Sapristi pompet! It's a giant Christmas puddding with a sign on top that says 'Low Bridge'.

GRYTPYPE Anything else?

MORIARTY Yes, a low bridge. This is our big chance!

GRYTPYPE   Big chance – to what?

MORIARTY   Ooh, to **eat!!!** Give me my teeth back!

GRYTPYPE   You can't have them, Moriarty, they're mine forever. You should never have left France for the National Health colonic irrigation!

MORIARTY   We must get to that pudding before Christmas or it will be out of date.

Moriarty

GRYTPYPE   Right, first we must stop them, Moriarty. Now, you stand in the road and raise your kilt. No! Not that much! It may be a lady driver.

FX   *Screeching tyres*

GRYTPYPE   Dear Moriarty, she pulled up –

MORIARTY   I know (*laughs*).

GRYTPYPE   (*laughing*) And I ruined the gag . . .

HARRY	And I'll continue as if nothing has happened.
BLUEBOTTLE	Oh, little thin man, are you ill?
MORIARTY	Yes! Only one thing can save poor old Moriarty's life.
GRYTPYPE	Yes, let me speak – I'm his guru – he **must** have a diet of **military** Christmas pudding, which he must eat on the move.
ECCLES	Oh, yer! Christmas pudding will keep you on the move all right.
BLUEBOTTLE	And we're driving one on the move.
GRYTPYPE	Good, help me get him and his starvation inside.
OMNES	*(grunting, etc)*
WALLACE	Elsewhere, the portion of the pudding destined for the Antarctic base was on board the SS Phyllis, going full steam ahead through the ice floes.
FX	*Wind and sea. Breaking of ice*
BLOODNOK	Gad, what a night on board – nothing but sleep. I tell you it's freezing out there. Mine are all shrivelled up!
SEAGOON	Keep your chin up, Major.
BLOODNOK	Why?
SEAGOON	It's in the soup.
BLOODNOK	I'm sorry, I thought my beard was on fire.

SEAMAN   Land ahead!

SEAGOON   They've sighted the ice shelf. Gad, in a few days we'll be at the base with the pudding. What a thrill it will be. I can see Dr Foulkes' face now.

BLOODNOK   You've got damned good eyesight.

SEAGOON   Prepare to unload pudding, dogs and sleds.

ORCHESTRA   *Dramatic chords*

FX   *Yapping dogs – grunting*

SEAGOON   It was hellish work pulling our pudding on the ice.

WALLACE   Seven months later as the crow flies, a line of dialogue.

BLOODNOK   Oh Seagoon, I'm knackered! What's the time?

SEAGOON   I can't tell until it gets dark.

BLOODNOK   Why?

SEAGOON   My watch has got a luminous dial.

BLOODNOK   Curse. We shall have to wait till nightfall before we know it's dark.

SEAGOON   Good God! We've run out of food!

BLOODNOK   We've still got the Christmas pudding.

SEAGOON   Stop! You touch that, Bloodnok, and I'll – That's for the boys at the Antarctic base.

BLOODNOK But if we don't eat it we won't have the strength to pull it.

SEAGOON I knew he was right. All right! Just a thin quarter-ounce slice each.

BLOODNOK Can't I have a **thick** quarter-ounce slice?

SEAGOON No, but I'll meet you halfway.

BLOODNOK All right, I'll see you there then.

ORCHESTRA *Dramatic chords*

FX *Icy wind — howling gale — distant howling wolves*

WALLACE Log of expedition.

FX	*Sound of nib scratching paper*
SEAGOON	December 52nd. Took off record of effects. (*FX cease*) For three nights now gallant Bloodnok has volunteered to stay awake and guard the pudding.
FX	*Sound of nib scratching paper*
BLOODNOK	December 1st. Pudding getting smaller.
FX	*Sound of nib scratching paper*
SEAGOON	Bloodnok getting bigger.
FX	*Scratchy nib as before*
BLOODNOK	Seagoon getting suspicious.
FX	*Scratchy nib*
SEAGOON	December 19th!
FX	*Writing as before*
BLOODNOK	Oo-ooh!
FX	*Writing*
SEAGOON	Caught Bloodnok red-handed digging into the pudding.
BLOODNOK	It's a lie! I'm brown handed!
SEAGOON	Bloodnok – you fool, you devil. Open your hand.
FX	*Coins hit floor*
SEAGOON	Ah, so that's what you're after. Threepenny bits!

BLOODNOK Yes, I wanted to make a phone call.

SEAGOON Phones? Here? Ha ha!

FX *Phone rings*

SEAGOON *(insane)* Don't answer it! It's – it's a mirage.

BLOODNOK Mirages don't ring – it's a phone.

SEAGOON You can't out-act me! It's – a – **PHONE!**

BLOODNOK Nonsense. (*Picks up phone*) Hello??

DISTORTED VOICE Hello, this is a mirage speaking.

FX *Phone crashed down*

BLOODNOK Oo-oh! You were right, Seagoon. Oh, unless we reach the base soon my mind will die of starvation!

FX *Duck quacks*

BLOODNOK It's the phone again – ohh!

SEAGOON Rubbish, ducks don't ring.

FX *Lorry drives up and stops*

ECCLES Hello, boys. We've brought you your Christmas pudding.

BLOODNOK It's a mirage!

SEAGOON What, what, what, what, what?

ECCLES Hello dere – phew, what a scorcher!

SEAGOON   The voice came from an idiot in a vest and sun helmet pouring with sweat.

ECCLES   Here, I bet this is the first time you've had snow in Libya.

BLOODNOK   **Libya??** It's a mirage –

SEAGOON   Nonsense! According to my calculations and our position on the map, we are twenty miles south of here.

BLOODNOK   Well, we shall soon settle this. Let's ask this mirage. Excuse me, sir, where's our position?

FRENCHMAN   Cher monsieur, soyez le bienvenu à New York.

BLOODNOK   He says, 'Welcome to New York'

SEAGOON   Nonsense. Mirages don't speak French.

ECCLES   What's New York doing in Libya?

BLOODNOK   You mean, what's New York doing in the Antarctic?

ECCLES   Wot's der Antarctic doing in Libya?

BLOODNOK   Perhaps it's on holiday.

ECCLES   This time of the year?

SEAGOON   Will you stop talking rubbish?

ECCLES   Have you got a piano?

BLOODNOK   Well, we'll soon settle where we are. I'll just toss this coin (*sound of coin spinning*). Ah. Heads! We are in Mongolia!

SEAGOON   Ah. But you're using a Mongolian penny.

BLOODNOK   Only one side.

SEAGOON   What does that mean?

BLOODNOK   It means, we're on one side of Mongolia.

ECCLES   I want to learn the piano.

SEAGOON   What are you talking about?

ECCLES   About ten words a minute

ALL THREE   (*Arguing*)

SEAGOON   Stop! Stop! – I know – it's **me** – **I'm** a mirage – that's it!
Help – help!!!

WALLACE   (*talks over Seagoon's babbling*) Ladies and gentlemen, you've
been listening to a series of mirages called the Goon
Show – it will be cold tonight with a frost.

ECCLES   Here, I found a piano –

FX   *Terrible piano fade out into Arctic winds – in the distance we hear Bloodnok
and Seagoon accusing each other of being a mirage.*

● ● ● ● ● ● ● ● ● ● ● ● ●

In control as ever – producer Dennis Main Wilson

BBC

▶ ▶ ▶ ▶ ▶ ▶ ▶ ▶ ▶ ▶ ▶ ▶ ▶ ▶ ▶

THE INTERNAL MOUNTAIN

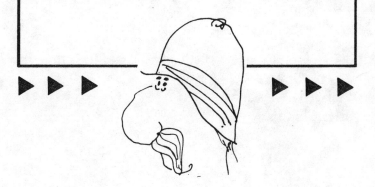

The Goon Show: 'Vintage Goons', No. 9
Recorded 16th February, 1958
First Transmission 28th December, 1986 (Radio 4)

Cast (main characters)

Spike Milligan
>The Spirit of Adventure
>Eccles
>Minnie Bannister
>Moriarty
>Jim Spriggs

Peter Sellers
>Cronk
>Henry Crun
>Grytpype
>Major Bloodnok
>Bluebottle

Harry Secombe
>Lord Hairy Seagoon

With The Ray Ellington Quartet, Max Geldray, and the Orchestra
conducted by Wally Stott.
Announcer Wallace Greenslade.
Producer Charles Chilton.

Ever in search of fresh adventures and new horizons, restless man of action Lord Hairy Seagoon sets himself the ultimate challenge: to climb Mount Everest *from the inside.* With a little ingenious help from Major Bloodnok, Seagoon succeeds in planting a Union Jack on the summit, only to find that there is truth in the old saying, 'It is better to travel hopefully than to arrive'.

WALLACE This is the BBC, natural inheritor of the alphabet ABC. Tonight's programme comes to you by arrangement with the makers of Kiddies Head Crushing Machines Ltd. We present Sita Fellers, Natty Floorcloth and Mike Middington in The Goon Show.

ORCHESTRA *Dramatic chords*

WALLACE This is a story of high adventure, one that will blaze its way across the lingth, length and longth of Great Britain, Ireland, Scotland, Wales, England and Scunthorpe.

HARRY This story will swell with pride the feet of every true Englishman, woman, child, cat, dog, chicken, to say nothing of Footo, the Wonder Boot Exploder!

FX *Explosion. Scream*

SPIKE Listeners may well ask what Footo the Wonder Boot Exploder has to do with our story. Well, **we shall see,** ha ha!

WALLACE Now to the drama. The –

HARRY Let me – the saga of The Internal Mountain.

▶ ▶ ▶ ▶ ▶ ▶ ▶ ▶ ▶ ▶ ▶ ▶ ▶ ▶ ▶

FX	*Chickens. Bagpipes. Splash. Chickens*
	Pause)
SPIKE	**We shall see.**
ORCHESTRA	*Dramatic chords*
SEAGOON	The Internal Mountain. Ha ha! How well I remember it. But first things first. My name is Lord Hairy Seagoon, Doctor of Philosophy and spinster of this parish. I am six foot three except on television. A man of action. Yes, I've rubbed shoulders with death. I've knocked on doors and run away. Oh, you may not believe this, I've run through Piccadilly without my underpants.
VOICE	*(gay)* You devil!
WALLACE	One night, as Lord Hairy lay tossing and turning in his egg box, under the stairs of Ronnie Scott's Jazz Club Anonymous – a mystic ethereal voice spoke to him.
GRAMS	*Harp – glissando*
GHOSTLY VOICE	Lord Seagoon, Seagoon. Can you hear me? Over.
SEAGOON	Yes, yes. I hear you strength three. Roger.
GHOSTLY VOICE	This is not Roger. It is Fred Toley, the spirit of adventure. Now living abroad owing to tax.
SEAGOON	*(laughing)* You sound like Milligan through a megaphone.
GHOSTLY VOICE	Listen, I come to gratify your desire. If you seek new horizons, climb Mount Everest.

▶ ▶ ▶ ▶ ▶ ▶ ▶ ▶ ▶ ▶ ▶ ▶ ▶ ▶

SEAGOON   Oh spirit there, it has already been clumbed.

GHOSTLY VOICE   It has not been clumbed from the **inside!**

SEAGOON   The **inside?** Oh spirit, you are right!

GHOSTLY VOICE   I must go now. I see my last tram coming.

SEAGOON   Wait, wait! Curses, the spirit has gone. It must have been only 70% proof. Climb Everest from the **inside?** It's never been done before. Cronk!

BBC

CRONK   Yes, my lord?

SEAGOON   Lay out my purple serge suit, yellow and black polka dot tie, green and mauve striped shirt, gold monogrammed boots, white bowler, and pink hand-painted souzaphone.

CRONK   Another funeral, sir?

SEAGOON   No, not today. I'm going to the Royal Alpine Club.

CRONK   I'll phone your office and tell them you won't be in.

SEAGOON   Yes, they'll have to try and manage without me.

FX   *Dialling phone number*

CRONK   Hello? Sir Bernard? Lord Seagoon's compliments, sir, he will not be in today.

FX   *Replaces phone*

SEAGOON   Well?

CRONK   You are fired, sir.

SEAGOON   Ha! Ha! I shouldn't worry about a job with my qualifications. Let them get another lift attendant.

CRONK   Spoken like a true failure.

SEAGOON   Mark my words, Cronk, he'll never get another man like me.

CRONK   That's what he said, sir. I never want another man like you.

SEAGOON   Is my horseless carriage ready?

CRONK	The chauffeur is pulling it here now.
FX	*Car horn*
ECCLES	Hello. The car's ready.
SEAGOON	Good lad, Eccles. Here's a sugar lump. That's what I like – car right outside my door.
ECCLES	Yer, but you never told me you lived on the twentieth floor.
SEAGOON	All right, Eccles – the Alpine Club.
FX	*Footsteps running away*
SEAGOON	I'd better follow him in the car.
FX	*Boots running away*
ORCHESTRA	*'The Lambeth Walk'*
WALLACE	With that inexplicable music, Seagoon arrives at the Royal Alpine Club.
FX	*Knocking on door*
CRUN	Kanchenjunga, 22,000 feet ...
FX	*Hammering on door*
MINNIE	Henry?
FX	*More hammering*
CRUN	What, Min?
MINNIE	There's someone knocking at the door.

Henry Crun

▶ ▶ ▶ ▶ ▶ ▶ ▶ ▶ ▶ ▶ ▶ ▶ ▶ ▶ ▶ ▶

CRUN   Which side, Min?

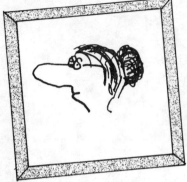

Minnie Bannister

MINNIE   Outside.

FX   *Knocking*

MINNIE   There it is again, Henry.

CRUN   He must be trying to get in.

SEAGOON   (*shouting*) Hello in there! I'm sorry, I happened to be knocking – I thought I'd call in.

CRUN   What is it, Min?

MINNIE   There was someone knocking at the door who thought he'd call in.

FX   *Door opens*

SEAGOON   Save your breath.

MINNIE   I have been saving it for years, it mounts up, you know.

CRUN   Please come in, whoever knocks.

SEAGOON   But I tell you –

CRUN Please don't interrupt the private affairs of the house. Is there someone knocking at the door?

SEAGOON *(shouting)* Yes!

CRUN *(shouting)* Who?

SEAGOON *(yells)* Me!

CRUN *(yells)* Then **come** in.

SEAGOON *(shouts)* I **am** in.

CRUN *(angry)* Then what are you knocking for?

SEAGOON *(furious)* I'm not knocking!
CRUN Then how do you expect us to know you're there? Who are you, little dwarf?

SEAGOON I'm Lord Seagoon.

CRUN It's Lord Seagoon, Min. What can we do for you, little dwarf?

SEAGOON I want the Alphine Club to cooperate in climbing Mount Everest from the inside.

CRUN Who would finance such a thing?

SEAGOON **Me**! Would you mind turning your back while I unfasten my money belt?

FX Padlock and chains. Hacksaw. Bolts being withdrawn. Creaking hinges

SEAGOON Oh – it was open all the time.

MINNIE   Can we turn round now?

SEAGOON   Yes. There is the money. Feast your eyes.

CRUN   Two shillings?

SEAGOON   Isn't that enough? I have another threepence in my boot, which I can explode with Footo the Wonder Boot Exploder.

CRUN   It's not enough. You'll need at least in the neighbourhood of a pound.

SEAGOON   A pound. It sounds like a rich neighbourhood.

CRUN   It is. I know a money lender there.

SEAGOON   A money lender? I suppose he works under a nom de plume?

CRUN   Yes, and in the summer the pong is terrible!

SEAGOON   I'll go and see him. Max Geldray – play me there on your nose support.

MAX   Ploogie

MAX AND ORCHESTRA   *Music*

WALLACE   The Internal Mountain Climbers, page 3, 4, 5, 6 and etc. Enter Seagoon in cloak, paper hat and hedgehog-skin jock strap. He approaches door of money lender and knocks.

FX   *Doorbell*

▶ ▶ ▶ ▶ ▶ ▶ ▶ ▶ ▶ ▶ ▶ ▶ ▶ ▶ ▶ ▶

Max Geldray

A heavily disguised Max Geldray, circa 1980

SEAGOON	Blast!
GRYTPYPE	Come in, Seagoon,
FX	*Door opens and closes*
SEAGOON	Good morning, nom de plume. I wish to borrow X pounds.
GRYTPYPE	X pounds? What for?
SEAGOON	X penses! Ha ha ha! Just my little joke.
FX	*Gunshot*
GRYTPYPE	Just my little bullet. Now, dear ragged Ned, sit on this blank cheque and tell me all.
SEAGOON	I want to borrow thirty thousand pounds.
FX	*Cascade of coins*
SEAGOON	All in farthings?
GRYTPYPE	Moriarty –
MORIARTY	What do you want, Grytpype, what do you want? Can't you see I'm busy painting the *Queen Elizabeth?*
GRYTPYPE	Parcel up the gentleman's money. Neddy, just sign this gentleman's agreement, please.
SEAGOON	Let me see it. (*Unfolds paper*) I promise to pay back thirty thousand pounds, plus **ten thousand?**

GRYTPYPE That's the tip, Neddy.

SEAGOON I refuse to sign.

GRAMS *Harp – ghostly glissando*

GHOSTLY VOICE Seagoon – I am the tooth fairy spirit come to help. Sign it with a false name.

SEAGOON Of course. Very well. (*Signs paper*) There. Miss Rita Body – that'll fool 'em.

GRYTPYPE So you're a woman?

SEAGOON (*high voice*) Yes.

MORIARTY My little darling, marry me! Ow ow!

SEAGOON Stop that! You'll go blind. Get him off – helppppp!

FX *Footsteps running away, getting faster and faster*

WALLACE By midnight Seagoon shook off Moriarty.

MORIARTY Thank you.

SEAGOON And the next part is the part where I say – tomorrow we sail for India.

FX *Ship's hooter*

JIM SPRIGGS Oh! And that's where you'll meet the great military mountaineer, Major Bloodnok.

ORCHESTRA *Dramatic chords*

FX *Gunfire, explosions*

▶ ▶ ▶ ▶ ▶ ▶ ▶ ▶ ▶ ▶ ▶ ▶ ▶ ▶ ▶ ▶

BLOODNOK   Oh dear – !!!

SEAGOON   You there!

BLOODNOK   Gad, look.

SEAGOON   Major Bloodnok?

BLOODNOK   The same. Late of the 3rd Heavy Herpes.

SEAGOON   This is the famous Eccles, late of the human race.

BLOODNOK   Eccles? Gad, it must be thirty years since we met.

ECCLES   I never met you before.

BLOODNOK   Then it must be longer!

▶ ▶ ▶ ▶ ▶ ▶ ▶ ▶ ▶ ▶ ▶ ▶ ▶ ▶ ▶

ECCLES   I wish mine was longer.

BLOODNOK   Of course. Well, now you're here, let me help you. Singhiz, take this gentleman's things and put them in the wicker basket marked Lot 23, 8 shillings o.n.o.

SEAGOON   Under the circumstances I'll be forced to stay with you.

BLOODNOK   Why?

SEAGOON   I'm skint.

BLOODNOK   Ah. Well, before you turn in, would you care for a nightcap?

SEAGOON   Yes.

BLOODNOK   Good – here's one with a chin strap, Now, how about a double brandy?

SEAGOON   Ah, no.

BLOODNOK   Rum?

SEAGOON   No.

BLOODNOK   Gin, then?

SEAGOON   Er – no.

BLOODNOK   Good heavens, man, haven't you got anything at all?

SEAGOON   I brought you this long thin green thing with several lumps held on by a bootlace tied round.

BLOODNOK   But I've already got one!

SEAGOON   How was I to know?

BLOODNOK   Isn't it obvious? You could have written!

SEAGOON   Would you mind holding this mangle? Thank you. Now, I'm here to offer you employment.

BLOODNOK   Work? Aaagh! (*Faints*)

FX   *Body and mangle hit floor*

SEAGOON   I got Bloodnok and the mangle onto his bed and revived hime with a glass of Footo the Wonder Boot Exploder.

FX   *Explosion – then another louder explosion*

BLOODNOK   Oh, that's better!

SEAGOON   Quick! Open the windows!

BLOODNOK   Now, tell me all –

SEAGOON   It's about klimbing Mount Everest from the inside ... (*fade*).

BLOODNOK   Klimbing, eh?

BOTH   (*ad lib, walking away*)

FX   *Construction work. Digging. Slaves singing work songs*

WALLACE   Work was begun on boring a hole up the middle of Everest.

BLOODNOK   Look at them – working like niggers!

SEAGOON   Bloodnok! That word is verboten.

▶ ▶ ▶ ▶ ▶ ▶ ▶ ▶ ▶ ▶ ▶ ▶ ▶ ▶ ▶ ▶

BLOODNOK	Look at 'em – working like verbotens. Now, surprise!
SEAGOON	What's this huge brown paper parcel?
BLOODNOK	A surprise from Blighty. It's a lift.
SEAGOON	A lift?
BLOODNOK	Yes, I'm going to have it built in to Mount Everest. Seagoon, you're going to travel up in style and comfort, lad. Let's unwrap it.
SEAGOON	I'm the strongest, I'll tear off the paper.
BLOODNOK	Nothing like tearing 'em off.
FX	*Tearing paper – ripping noises*
BLOODNOK	There we are. Now let's see what it's like inside.
FX	*Lift door opens*
MINNIE	Oh, thank heaven. Is this ladies' lingerie?
BLOODNOK	No, it's wogs galore and loin cloths. Wait! Is it – it's Minnie Bannister! Minnie Bannister, the darling of Roper's Light Horse and the 3rd Foot and Mouth.
MINNIE	The same.
BLOODNOK	Oh, fair dear little creature. Don't you recognise me?
MINNIE	Dennis – Dennis Bloodnok! Were the tests clear?
BLOODNOK	Oh my treasure, you little beauty. (*Kissing hand*) Your little hand – let me take your ring off so I can kiss it. (*Kisses*)

MINNIE	Oooh-ooh.
BLOODNOK	Remember Poona – the Governor's balls in 1927?
MINNIE	I'll never forget them.
BLOODNOK	What was that waltz?
BLOODNOK & MINNIE	*(sing)* 'I was born in Vienna, Where the girls and the men are, So exceedingly all bright and gay, and I blow away. . .' *(They fade away)*
SEAGOON	With eyes closed they danced in ecstasy . . . over a clif
BLOODNOK & MINNIE	*(sing their way back)*
SEAGOON	And back again.
BLOODNOK	Greenslade, take Madame Bannister to my tent.
WALLACE	Yes.
BLOODNOK	Not much of a part. There she goes, sweet Min Bann. looks exactly the same as when I first met her – blood terrible.
FX	*Whistle*
BLOODNOK	Offside! Everyone back to their own beds.
FX	*Footsteps running away*
SEAGOON	You fool, Bloodnok, that's the danger whistle. The me are going to start blasting.
BLOODNOK	Rude words cannot hurt me, lad.

▶ ▶ ▶ ▶ ▶ ▶ ▶ ▶ ▶ ▶ ▶ ▶ ▶ ▶ ▶ ▶

SEAGOON   I'd better check that everyone has taken cover.
Bluebottle?

FX   *Approaching running footsteps*

BLUEBOTTLE   I heard you call, I am coming, my Captain. I was over
there eating my jelly babies in private – you get more that
way.

SEAGOON   Bluebottle, run in the tunnel and see if all the men are
out.

BLUEBOTTLE   Your wish is my command. I will do that, Captain. I'm
not afraid. I will. (*Pause*) I say, Captain – there's a dirty
big stick of dynamite in there.

SEAGOON   You're perfectly safe – it's a long fuse.

BLUEBOTTLE   I knew it would be safe. I trust my Captain. He always
tells me the truth. (*Pause*) You are telling the truth –
aren't you?

Spike Milligan

SEAGOON	Yes – off you go.
FX	*Footsteps running away*
SEAGOON	There he goes, brave, tall, straight as a hockey stick and twice as thin. Even as I speak he enters the dreaded tunnel.
BLUEBOTTLE	Hello? (*Echo*) Hello, everybody. Is anybody in there? Is anyone still in the tunnel? If so, you must leave. You have ten minutes before the dynamite –
FX	*Colossal explosion – falling bits, knife, fork, spoon, marbles etc.*
BLUEBOTTLE	You rotten swine, you! You've shredded my best trousers and melted my Milky Way. Ahhh!
SEAGOON	Quick, Ellington, the coup de grâce!
QUARTET	*Music*
BLOODNOK	That night my mangle and I were so excited I didn't feel tired, so I slept with my eyes open. When I awoke, my eyes were closed. So I must have dozed off when I was asleep with my eyes shut open. Eh?
SEAGOON	You have an unsound mind.
BLOODNOK	Unsound? Hit it with this hammer.
FX	*Hammer. Wallop – loud bonggg*
BLOODNOK	Dinner is served
SEAGOON	Just hold this mangle.
ECCLES	Hello – I tought I heard der sound of a mind.

▶ ▶ ▶ ▶ ▶ ▶ ▶ ▶ ▶ ▶ ▶ ▶ ▶ ▶ ▶ ▶

BLOODNOK   Eccles, why do people take an instant dislike to me?

ECCLES   It saves time!

BLOODNOK   Just hold this mangle.

BEARER   Excuse me, camel's waiting to take us to foot Mount Everest.

ECCLES   The foot? I didn't know Everest had a foot?

BLOODNOK   Yes – it's got more – see here, Everest 29,000 feet.

ECCLES   That's a centipede.

BLOODNOK   Well, it had to go some where. Now, Seagoon, could you oblige me? Say, five pounds?

SEAGOON   Say five pounds? Right – five pounds!

BLOODNOK   Thank you!

SEAGOON   Have **you** five pounds, Eccles?

ECCLES   No. Have you got five pounds, Major?

BLOODNOK   Well, you look like a sporting man. There.

ECCLES   Ah. There, Neddy.

SEAGOON   Thanks. Here you are, Bloodnok.

BLOODNOK   Oh, thank you.

ECCLES   Just hold this mangle.

ORCHESTRA   *Corny music hall chord*

WALLACE	That appears to be the end of that corny routine. Now, the sound of camels.
FX	*Camels. Strange rumbling sounds — raspberries*
SEAGOON	We rode in silence, save for the odd noises camels are wont to make – or was it Bloodnok?
FX	*Explosion*
BLOODNOK	Oh, that curry! It was hell back there, I tell you.
SEAGOON	(*laughing*) It's hell back here!
WALLACE	Didn't you finally arrive at the mountain and find the lift installed and get in it?
SEAGOON	You can tell we're getting near the end.
JIM SPRIGGS	All get in the elevator. Going up.
FX	*Elevator ascending*
BLOODNOK	Fancy – the first men to go up Everest from the inside. Just hold this mangle.
FX	*Elevator*
JIM SPRIGGS	Three thousand feet.
FX	*Elevator*
JIM SPRIGGS	Four thousand feet
FX	*Elevator. Long, long pause*
SEAGOON	Look, this is terribly boring for the listeners.
BLOODNOK	Yes! But what can one do in a lift?

▶ ▶ ▶ ▶ ▶ ▶ ▶ ▶ ▶ ▶ ▶ ▶ ▶ ▶ ▶

JIM SPRIGGS	You can hold this mangle.
SEAGOON	Spriggs, sing them a song.
JIM SPRIGGS	All right.
FX	*Long piano introduction*
JIM SPRIGGS	(*starts to sing*) I –
BLOODNOK	It's all right, we're here now!

SEAGOON	Hand me the flag. I claim this Union Jack for England! Well, what do you think, Bloodnok?
BLOODNOK	Hardly worth it for the view. Hold this mangle. (*Long pause*)
WALLACE	Good God – they've finished.

Jack Oakley

Announcer Wallace Greenslade to the fore

THE SILENT BUGLER

The Goon Show: 'Vintage Goons', No. 10
Recorded 23rd February, 1958
First Transmission 29th December, 1986 (Radio 4)

Cast (main characters)

Spike Milligan
    'M'
    Sergeant Eccles
    Minnie Bannister

Peter Sellers
    Vanderschmidt
    Ticket Collector
    Colonel Brollicks
    Henry Crun
    Major Bloodnok
    Bluebottle

Harry Secombe
    Captain Hairy Seagoon (Agent X2)

Ray Ellington
    Airline official
    Russian

With The Ray Ellington Quartet, Max Geldray, and the Orchestra
conducted by Wally Stott.
Script by Spike Milligan.
Announcer Wallace Greenslade.
Producer Charles Chilton.

◆ ◆ ◆ ◆ ◆ ◆ ◆ ◆ ◆ ◆ ◆ ◆ ◆ ◆

Armed with a rubber dagger and a set of disguises that includes a ginger thermal beard, reversible plastic socks, and false cardboard skis, Agent X2 (alias Captain Hairy Seagoon) sets off on the trail of a Russian master spy (alias The Silent Bugler). However, despite such technologically advanced accessories, it is Bloodnok's plain old-fashioned undergarments which finally save our hero from a death worse than fate . . .

WALLACE The BBC presents Agents Sellers, Secombe and Milligan in the – er – the – er – (*Whispers*) Look, I'm new here . . .

SECOMBE (*whispers*) Here – on this paper . . .

WALLACE The Goat Show. (*Whispers*) You sure this is right?

SECOMBE We'll have to get another typist – it's really The Goon Show and –

ORCHESTRA *Awful chord*

WALLACE This is getting silly. Ahem – today, in the American Senate, Senator Vanderschmidt said –

VANDERSCHMIDT (*powerful American accent*) Money!

WALLACE And he continued by saying –

VANDERSCHMIDT Hearn. Hearn. Hearn. (*Fades*) Money – hearn hearn – money.

WALLACE In response on March 3rd in the House of Commons at four o'clock, the Prime Minister said –

PM Tea?

FX	*Mad rush of politicians stampeding for canteen – cries of TEA! TEA! CAKE! CAKE!*
WALLACE	These ev – (*he is interrupted by the orchestra*)
ORCHESTRA	*Terrible chord*
WALLACE	These everyday exchanges in our political circles are made known to us all by the daily newspoppers – tsk tsk. But what of the secret services?
SPIKE	Yes indeed, what of them? (*Embarrassing pause*)
WALLACE	Oh, I didn't know you'd finished – it's got engaged on the door. We give you now only one story of only one minute fragment in this mosaic of political intrigue. Take the case of Agent X2. (*Fade*)
SEAGOON	I am X2. My miss – (*He is interrupted by the orchestra*)
ORCHESTRA	*Dramatic chord*
SEAGOON	For God's sake! My mission started when I was called to HQ M15. I was disguised as a commuter, but I'd hardly got on board the train when I had the uneasy feeling I was being followed – a man in uniform –
FX	*Train door slides open*
SEAGOON	He approached me with something in his hand.
COLLECTOR	Tickets, please.
SEAGOON	Oh yes!
COLLECTOR	This is a platform ticket.

◆ ◆ ◆ ◆ ◆ ◆ ◆ ◆ ◆ ◆ ◆ ◆

SEAGOON   That's right, I always travel by platform.

COLLECTOR   Where's your ticket?

SEAGOON   Just joking. Here we are.

COLLECTOR   I know we're here, but where's your ticket?

SEAGOON   There.

COLLECTOR   Wait a minute, this ticket's from Dover to Melbourne, Steerage Class – this is the Central Line Tube.

SEAGOON   April Fool!

COLLECTOR This is December!

SEAGOON Oh, my calendar must be slow. There. My ticket.

COLLECTOR This ticket was issued in 1902.

SEAGOON Really? Gad, we're running late.

COLLECTOR And it's for the Brighton to London stagecoach.

SEAGOON Yes, indeed.

COLLECTOR This ain't a bloody stagecoach, mate.

SEAGOON You mean this train isn't horsedrawn? I demand my money back.

COLLECTOR You **got** to **pay** for the **ticket.** Where did you get on?

SEAGOON *(aside)* Curse! The game's up. *(Aloud)* Where was that last station?

COLLECTOR Clapham Junction.

SEAGOON That's it. That's where I got on.

COLLECTOR We didn't stop there.

SEAGOON You think it was easy?

COLLECTOR Where are you going to?

SEAGOON The next station.

COLLECTOR Right, that'll be eighteen shillings and threepence.

FX *Coins – cascades of them*

SEAGOON   Sorry, it's all in farthings.

COLLECTOR   Thank you.

FX   *Door closes*

SEAGOON   Fool. Little does he know that the real fare is not eighteen and threepence, but thirty-two pounds six shillings.

COLLECTOR   Little does he know that I'm nothing to do with the railway at all.

ORCHESTRA   *Boom-boom chord*

WALLACE   Thus Seagoon arrived at HQ M15, with the wind behind him.

FX   *Raspberry. Door opens*

'M'   *(upper class twit)* Ah, come in X2. Now, you **know** what we want you for.

A Twit

SEAGOON No.

'M' Oh dear. Well, don't go away. We'll think of **something.** Ever been to Russia?

SEAGOON No – but I've been to Scunthorpe.

'M' That'll do. Colonel Brollicks, will you explain to him?

BROLLICKS Yes, well, we have reason to believe that the Russians have perfected a time machine. With it they could go forward into the future; once there they'd build planes that would travel faster than the speed of light. They've **got** to be stopped doing such a thing. You're the man for the job.

SEAGOON Oh, ta!

BROLLICKS Thank you. Are you married?

SEAGOON No, sir. I want to remain celibate.

BROLLICKS Understandable. Then marry a nun. Now, I would go on this mission myself, but, well, it's too dangerous.

SEAGOON You mean, I might get killed?

BROLLICKS Let me put it this way – yes.

FX *Door opens*

'M' Ah, Mr Crun! Mr –

CRUN Ahhh – Go – go – good mor – mor – mor – morning.

'M' Morning. This man hiding under the table is X2. Would you go under and brief him?

CRUN Ah! Go – go – good mor – mor – morning, Mi – Mi – Mister – Mister –

SEAGOON Mister Captain Hairy Seagoon at your service, sir.

CRUN Ah yes, Mister Captain Seagoonatyourservicesir. Now, here is a photo of the Russian master spy, Igor Blimey. He's escaped from every prison camp in Europe.

SEAGOON There's nothing on this photograph.

CRUN He's escaped again! They call him, the Silent Bugler.

SEAGOON The **Silent** Bugler?

CRUN Nobody has ever seen him. But here is a rare record of him.

FX *Record goes on – no sound, only surface hiss*

SEAGOON I can't hear anything.

CRUN That's him! The Silent Bugler. If you ever hear anything like **that**, be on your guard.

SEAGOON With that warning ringing in my teeth, I spent the next three weeks training to listen to silences under Major Bloodnok.

ORCHESTRA *'Bloodnok Theme'*

FX *Explosions*

BLOODNOK   Aah, ooh! Batman? A clean pair and hurry! Now, you were saying, Mister Captain Seagoonatyourservice?

SEAGOON   I said, during the last war they say you were taken prisoner.

BLOODNOK   Yes, yes, but I escaped.

SEAGOON   Where from?

BLOODNOK   Dartmoor. Now, first of all your disguises. Stand by to check. One ginger thermal beard with detachable bells and suppositories.

SEAGOON   Yes.

BLOODNOK   One pair of reversible plastic socks easily convertible to dog cardigan or bust of Marilyn Monroe.

SEAGOON   Yes

BLOODNOK   One pair of false cardboard skis. One fur-lined wicker teapot with underwater escape apparatus and view of the Matterhorn.

SEAGOON   Yes.

BLOODNOK   One rubber dagger.

SEAGOON   What's the use of a rubber dagger?

◆ ◆ ◆ ◆ ◆ ◆ ◆ ◆ ◆ ◆ ◆ ◆ ◆

BLOODNOK We don't want to shed blood needlessly. Now, finance. Three thousand lire in rupees, payable in pesetas at any Mongolian bank whilst wearing tennis shoes in a thunderstorm during an equinox of the moon.

SEAGOON That'll do nicely.

BLOODNOK Now, the sensitivity test. I shall just blindfold you. Now, I want you to tell me what I'm doing. Right?

SEAGOON Er, you're taking my gold ring off my finger.

BLOODNOK Yes, yes, yes.

SEAGOON Now you're removing my gold watch. And my fountain pen from my pocket.

BLOODNOK Bravo, keep it up.

SEAGOON Now you're taking my wallet. And my money belt – now you're tying me to a chair –

BLOODNOK (*from distance*) Keep going.

SEAGOON I can't feel you doing anything now. Hello, Major? Major? Hello – Hello – . . . you **SWINE!**

ORCHESTRA *Awful chords again*

WALLACE That appears to be the end of The Silent Bugler, Part One. Now a smile, a harmonica, a large nose – Max Geldray.

MAX AND *Music*
ORCHESTRA

WALLACE Now, the Si –

ORCHESTRA *Awful chords*

WALLACE The Silent Bugler, Part Two? How time flies. First, for listeners who have just tuned in, here is a rapid synopsis.

FX *Run first part of show at high speed, slow down to hear Seagoon say 'you SWINE!'*

WALLACE Now read on.

◆ ◆ ◆ ◆ ◆ ◆ ◆ ◆ ◆ ◆ ◆ ◆

SEAGOON Before my departure for Russia, I took one final test.

BROLLICKS We want you to identify objects that will be held up in rapid succession. Sergeant Eccles, do your duty.

ECCLES OK. The first object I hold up is **this.**

SEAGOON It's a banana!

ECCLES Good, good. (*Eats it*) Dat got rid of that. Now then, what's this?

SEAGOON A pencil.

 FX Sound of man eating pencil

ECCLES Good. (*Gulps*) And dat got rid of dat! What's this (*grunting and straining*) that I'm holding?

SEAGOON Er, let me see . . .

ECCLES Hurry up – I can't hold it up all day! **Come on!** Look at the shape.

 FX Creaking noises as of something about to give way

SEAGOON Yes. I've seen one like it. Er – no, I'm not quite sure. I give up. What is it?

ECCLES It's an elephant.

FX	*Eccles drops elephant*
SEAGOON	Ah, of course – he was the big one.
ECCLES	Ohh. I didn't know he had a big one.
BROLLICKS	Now, Seagoon, just one more small thing. Private Bluebottle.
BLUEBOTTLE	Sir! I heard you call, sir Captain, I heard you. Hello, everybody and sir. Like a jelly baby?
BROLLICKS	No thank you, baby.
SEAGOON	I understand you have a secret weapon for me.
BLUEBOTTLE	I have it, I have. Unscrews false kneecap, takes out secret gun. Am in agony, as I have not got false kneecap. Puts on bold face. It still hurts, though.
SEAGOON	Oh, what is it?
BLUEBOTTLE	It is my backshot pistol.
SEAGOON	You mean, whoever fires the pistol gets killed himself?
BLUEBOTTLE	Yes. You just give it to the enemy, he aims at you, and then – bang! – he gets deaded himself! He he he!
SEAGOON	How does it work?

◆ ◆ ◆ ◆ ◆ ◆ ◆ ◆ ◆ ◆ ◆ ◆

BLUEBOTTLE I'll show you. I just point the gun at you, then I pull the trigger and – ah hah! No! **You** point it at **me,** and **you** pull the trigger.

SEAGOON So. I·point it at you like this.

BLUEBOTTLE **No!** Don't point it at **me,** point it at **yourself** – I think –

SEAGOON But you said –

FX *Gunshot*

BLUEBOTTLE (*screams*) You rotten swine you – right in my hat, look at the hole! People can see in now and laugh at my school hair cut! (*Seagoon and Bluebottle walk away, Seagoon comforting him*)
(*Silence*)

WALLACE Oh! The Silent Bugler, Part Three. Sorry, took me by suprise.

PETER In a dark car wearing a frilly hat with the brim well over the headlights, Seagoon was driven to a submerged airport.

FX *Plane on tarmac, engine running*

WALLACE (*announcing through bull horn*) Will all passengers with a disguised M15 ticket for mystery flight X to undisclosed destination, please inflate their false wigs and crawl as inconspicuously as possible to the isolated black plane standing in the shadow of the barbed wire. Thank you.

OFFICIAL   Mystery flight X, this way, please. Passports, please. Name?

BLOODNOK   Mrs Gladys Murgatroyd, widow and go go dancer with walnuts.

OFFICIAL   Right, next.

ECCLES   Woof woof, growl, woof.

FX   *Stamping passport*

OFFICIAL   Right, next.

Spike Milligan

WALLACE   Just an old BBC announcer.

OFFICIAL   Good luck. Next.

FX   *Rubber stamp*

PETER   Sir Arthur Brogglers, child molester and plumber.

FX   *Rubber stamp*

OFFICIAL   (*screams*) Oh! my finger!!!

PETER   Little does he know I am not Sir Arthur Brogglers child molester and plumber but – Dick Scratcher.

ECCLES   Little does he know that I am not woof woof, growl, but growl, woof woof.

BLOODNOK   Little do they know that I am not Mrs Gladys Murgatroyd, widow and go go dancer, but Secret Agent X.

OFFICIAL   Now you, sir?

SEAGOON   I am X2, or Captain Hairy Seagoon. Secret British agent.

OFFICIAL   Ha ha ha! You – **you** a secret agent? (*Reels away in fits of laughter*)

SEAGOON   Plainly he didn't believe me.

◆ ◆ ◆ ◆ ◆ ◆ ◆ ◆ ◆ ◆ ◆ ◆ ◆

OFFICIAL   Close bulkhead doors. Fasten your safety belts, please.

MINNIE   Morning.

OMNES   Morning.

FX   *Plane starts to move away*

MINNIE   Morning, everybody. Everybody take your seats please. All safety belts to be fastened. Come, Captain Seagoon, you **must** fasten your belt now.

SEAGOON   Why?

MINNIE   Your trousers are coming down. Now, don't be nervous, flying isn't dangerous – **crashing** is dangerous.

FX   *Plane takes off*

QUARTET   Music

SEAGOON   By now I was deep in enemy territory. Very very deep. I was dropped without a parachute. Walking along the Fredstrasse in Dresden I was halted by two men heavily disguised as Englishmen.

BLOODNOK   Good morgen, Herr Seagoon. And how is mein herr this morning?

SEAGOON   Going a bit thin on top.

BLOODNOK   Achtung, Spitfire, egg in the eye, Rommel, gezeitung, up the old gelingen blar . . .

SEAGOON   (*aside*) I **must** reply. Ahem. Si si signor. (*Aside*) Poor German fool. Little do they know that I am **not** really a German, but I speak the language fluently.

BLOODNOK   Poor German fool. Little does he know that I am not a poor German fool, but Major Bloodnok, a poor English fool.

ECCLES   Pardon, mein herr, gute morgen . . .

FX   *Austrian cuckoo clock*

SEAGOON   Ach, Himmel! Ten to one – time to open my sealed orders.

BLOODNOK   Two twenty – time to open my sealed orders.

ECCLES   Twenty to three – time to open my sealed orders.

SEAGOON   It says, The man standing before you is Major Bloodnok X.

BLOODNOK   Mine says, The man standing before you is Captain Seagoon X2, who has just been informed who **you** are.

ECCLES   Mine says, Beat two eggs, add four ounces of flour . . . Ooh, it's Mrs Beeton's Cookery Book.

◆ ◆ ◆ ◆ ◆ ◆ ◆ ◆ ◆ ◆ ◆ ◆

BLOODNOK   X2?

SEAGOON   X?

ECCLES   Er – two x and bacon!

BLOODNOK   We shall meet here when the clock strikes one.

SEAGOON   Right.

FX   *Clock strikes one*

SEAGOON   Bloodnok!

BLOODNOK   Seagoon!

ECCLES   Two x and bacon

FX   *Bloodnok and Seagoon hitting Eccles*

BLOODNOK   That's enough, we'll save him for later.

FX   *Phone rings*

BLOODNOK   Don't answer that phone! It's ringing in Russian!

SEAGOON   Don't worry, I'll put on this false thermal beard. Now. Hello? Who's speaking?

WALLACE   If you take that bloody silly beard off, I'll tell you. Now listen, this is HQ M15. Orders. The location of the time machine is in the Dresden Opera House.

ECCLES   I can't sing a note.

SEAGOON   Shut up! Men, the Dresden Opera House, hurry.

◆ ◆ ◆ ◆ ◆ ◆ ◆ ◆ ◆ ◆ ◆ ◆

FX   *Men streaking away – fade out then fade back*

BLOODNOK   (*breathless*) Ah, here we are – exhausted. What's this say? Today's symphony concert featuring – *Relgub Tneliseht?*

SEAGOON   Gad, that spells the Silent Bugler backwards.

FX   *Orchestra tuning up*

ECCLES   Ah, here's an empty box. Not a match left in it.

BLOODNOK   We're just in time to miss the first movements.

SEAGOON   Look at the orchestra. They must be all of a hundred and fifty.

ECCLES   Some look much younger.

SEAGOON   Shut up, and listen.

GRAMS   *Opening of 'Unfinished Symphony'*

SEAGOON   I wonder which one is the Silent Bugler.

BLOODNOK   That's him. Curse, he's stopped playing.

SEAGOON   I didn't hear him.

BLOODNOK   Well, listen – there he is now.

SEAGOON   Where, where?

BLOODNOK   Blast, he's gone again.

SEAGOON   What was that? The music seemed to repeat.

BLOODNOK   I didn't notice anything, and I know my Wagner backwards.

SEAGOON   They're not playing it backwards.

GRAMS   *Music slows down like a gramophone record winding down*

SEAGOON   Good heavens, the orchestra's **miming** to a gramophone record – another BBC economy!

BLOODNOK   Then the Silent Bugler –

SEAGOON   He doesn't exist – it must be all a bluff.

BLOODNOK   You mean –

SEAGOON   The whole orchestra are secret Russian agents. We must get out of here quick.

ECCLES   But the time machine?

◆ ◆ ◆ ◆ ◆ ◆ ◆ ◆ ◆ ◆ ◆ ◆

SEAGOON   We must split up.

ECCLES   How do I split up?

SEAGOON   Shut up! We must split up and search under the theatre.
Wait – (*slowly*) – how do I know you're both not enemy
agents? Your identity cards, please.

BLOODNOK   My card.

SEAGOON   (*reads*) Major D. Bloodnok. My card.

BLOODNOK   (*reads*) Captain H. Seagoon.

ECCLES   My card!

BLOODNOK   (*reads*) The two of clubs.

FX   *Eccles being hit*

WALLACE   Here is a short résumé of what you're missing on TV:

PETER   Helen Lovejoy, beautiful heiress to the Halibut millions,
has been jilted at the altar by Villion de Paprikon, one
legged son of Louis XIV. Peter, Villion's Eton boating
friend has heard this, but being in Tibet not as loud, and
he has embarrassed Mary, his fiancée, who being the only
cousin of Sir Ray Ellington has caught it off Dick
Scratcher and has passed the title on to Baron Geldray,
also heir to the Halibut oil millions.

WALLACE   Have you finished?

FX   *Voices echo from now on*

BLOODNOK   We are alone under the theatre.

◆ ◆ ◆ ◆ ◆ ◆ ◆ ◆ ◆ ◆ ◆ ◆ ◆

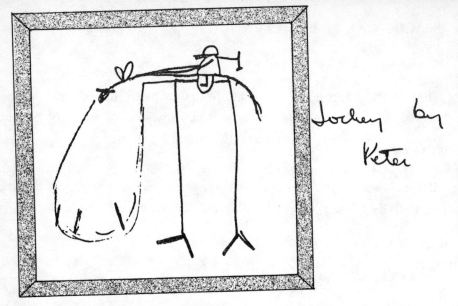

Jockey by
Peter

SEAGOON	Look! The time machine.
ECCLES	It says half past four.
SEAGOON	Shut up!
BLOODNOK	I'll just put this bomb under it – stand back –
FX	*Immediate explosion*
BLOODNOK	Could have done with a longer fuse.
ECCLES	Is dat why we're up in the air?
SEAGOON	Somebody's coming!
RUSSIAN	Come down from up there! Hands up in Russian!
BLOODNOK	The KGB! Run for it in English.
FX	*Footsteps running away followed by bullets whizzing past*

SEAGOON   Taxi!

FX   *Taxi screeches to a halt — then races off. Fast car. Horses. Train. Jet plane. Bus. Screeching brakes.*

ECCLES   We've made it.

SEAGOON   Safe at last.

RUSSIAN   So, you all came back. Hands up in Russian again. Up, down. Up, down. When we take prisoners we like them fit!

BLOODNOK   Too late, Ruskie — we destroyed your time machine. We can die knowing we've done our job.

ECCLES   Wot you mean, **we**?

SEAGOON   Shut up!

RUSSIAN   You fools!

ECCLES   Tell us something new.

RUSSIAN   You only destroyed a replica of the time machine.

SEAGOON   Curse. Foiled by an unpatriotic script.

BLOODNOK   (*whispers*) Wait. I happen to be wearing red flannel underdrawers. If I could lower my trousers, he'll salute!

SEAGOON   I'll pull from the back. One, two, three.

FX   *Ripping material*

RUSSIAN   Ah — I salute our glorious flag. Long live Russia!

BLOODNOK   Get him!

SEAGOON   OK Ruskie, hands up, down, up, down – knees bend, bend – stretch, on the spot running – begin!

RUSSIAN   (*gasping*) Don't shoot. I tell you where time machine is – page 33!

FX   *Rapid turning of pages*

SEAGOON   Right. No mistakes this time. Put this bomb under it – it's timed to go off on the 23rd November.

BLOODNOK   That's my birthday!

SEAGOON   (*sing*) Happy birthday to –
and ECCLES

FX   *Explosion. Disappearing screams as our heroes are blown up*

WALLACE   Well, that's that – will the last person out please lock up.

ORCHESTRA   *Awful chords*

Jack Oakley

Ray Ellington sings, Max Geldray (left) watches

BBC

THE DREADED PIANO CLUBBER

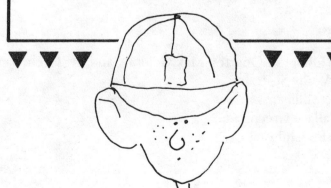

The Goon Show: 'Vintage Goons', No. 12
Recorded 9th March, 1958
First Transmission Boxing Day, 1986 (Radio 4)

Cast (main characters)

Spike Milligan
Dudley Pringe
Sergeant
Minnie Bannister
Eccles
Count Moriarty

Peter Sellers
Henry Crun
Captain Bluebottle
William Cobblers
Churchill
Grytpype

Harry Secombe
Constable Ned Seagoon

Wallace Greenslade
The Judge

With The Ray Ellington Quartet, Max Geldray, and the Orchestra
conducted by Wally Stott.
Script by Spike Milligan.
Announcer Wallace Greenslade.
Producer Charles Chilton.

▼ ▼ ▼ ▼ ▼ ▼ ▼ ▼ ▼ ▼ ▼ ▼ ▼ ▼ ▼

It was a foggy winter's night when the Piano Clubber struck down his first innocent victim, a Mr Henry Crun. Young Constable Ned Seagoon of the River Police was quickly on the scene, but it was not until some fifty years later that he at last tracked down the elusive Clubber, and faced his quarry in a final showdown . . .

WALLACE   In an endeavour to prove that radio is not blind we present after a successful season at Rowton House, another programme in the series, which by careful planning, meticulous writing and superb presentation has managed to avoid winning the Radio Award. Peter Sellers, Harry Secombe and Spike Milligan in –

HARRY   It's my turn – ahem. The Goon Show.

FX   *Very badly played, out-of-tune piano during which it falls to pieces*

PRINGE   Good evening. My name is Dudley Pringe, contemporary armchair detective and trainee plumber. Tonight from my case book I'd like to tell you the story of a krim that shook England. To tell you more is a man who remembers it all.

HARRY   (*upper class twit*) Thank you, Dudley, thank you. I'm **not** the man who remembers it all, so I'll step down. Thank you.

WALLACE   Thank you. Every now and again, there occurs a krim that makes us sit up, others sit down, some stand and face East – it all depends.

▼ ▼ ▼ ▼ ▼ ▼ ▼ ▼ ▼ ▼ ▼ ▼

PRINGE   For some time now the Goons have had access to Scotland Yard's secret files – thanks to an arrangement with the police known as Dropsy Bill, because he has dropsy.

PETER   (*American 'March of Time' voice*) From these confidential files comes a story that no Sunday newspaper would dare to print as it hasn't got big tits. The story of – The Dreaded Piano Clubber.

GRAMS   *Same awful piano accompanied by orchestra ends in argument between pianist and conductor*

FX   *Big Ben chimes. Fog horn. Footsteps of bobby on the beat*

WALLACE   On such a foggy night an English bobby walks his beat.

FX   *Loud 'klunk' as man walks into lamp post*

ECCLES   Oh –

SEAGOON   It was such a winter's night as this when **I**, Constable Ned Seagoon of Long Division, London River Police, joined the river police.

FX   *Splash as body falls in water. Wading through water*

SEAGOON   I'll be glad when we get a launch, Sergeant.

SERGEANT   It is a bit chilly on the truncheon, I must say. Still, we must guard our great river Thames.

SEAGOON   Yes. We'd better walk up the Embankment and get dry before we go in again.

FX   *Piano*

▼ ▼ ▼ ▼ ▼ ▼ ▼ ▼ ▼ ▼ ▼ ▼ ▼

SERGEANT	What was that noise?
SEAGOON	It sounded like a piano. I'll make a note!
FX	*One piano note*
SERGEANT	It's already made one.
FX	*Piano falling on a man. Shattering noise and groans*
SEAGOON	It came from over there – points.
FX	*Footsteps running away, then back*
SEAGOON	Look, a body in the gutter. Quick, Sergeant, take down this description. Five feet two short, tubby, wearing blue trousers and jacket, good looking.
SERGEANT	Right.
SEAGOON	That takes care of me. Now, the body. Wearing city suit, flattened bowler hat and bowler trousers. Carrying ear trumpet, side whiskers, bald. Sex, male.
SERGEANT	Search his pockets, Jim.
FX	*Jingling coins*
SEAGOON	Five pounds.
SERGEANT	Oh, thank you, sir!
SEAGOON	Not a word to the Inspector or he'll want some.
SERGEANT	The crook!
SEAGOON	Here's a birth certificate in his hip pocket. Gad,

▼ ▼ ▼ ▼ ▼ ▼ ▼ ▼ ▼ ▼ ▼ ▼

according to this, his hip pocket is a hundred and thirty years old. So this might not be murder after all, this man might have died from natural causes.

SERGEANT I don't think he died from either, Jim.

SEAGOON Why not?

SERGEANT He's getting up, Jim.

CRUN Aah-aaaah-aaaaah.

SEAGOON Have you got all that down, Sergeant?

SERGEANT Yes, sir.

SEAGOON Easy, old man.

CRUN Where am I?

SEAGOON England, sir.

CRUN England?

OMNES (*sing*) 'There'll Always Be An England ...'

SEAGOON What happened, sir?

CRUN I fainted.

SEAGOON Fainted – when?

CRUN Just after a man struck me down with a piano.

SEAGOON Struck – with a piano? Is that what these bits are?

CRUN Some of them are mine.

SEAGOON   A piano? Clubbed with a piano? Did you get the number of the instrument?

CRUN   No, he had his lights out. But I can describe the man.

SEAGOON   Good. Take this down.

SERGEANT   Right, sir.

CRUN   He was wearing turquoise trousers.

SERGEANT   How do you spell turquoise?

SEAGOON   I don't.

SERGEANT   I'll just pronounce it.

CRUN   A shirt, a tie, a jacket, a hat, socks, and one pair of shoes.

SEAGOON   Splendid. With that description, if ever he enters a nudist colony he's a gonner. Anything else?

CRUN   Yes, he was carrying a piano, and this recording of Max Geldray.

MAX AND ORCHESTRA   *Music (It ends with piano falling on him)*

FX   *Disintegrating piano. Screams. Police whistles*

WALLACE   That was the second time the Piano Clubber struck. In the months to come he struck twenty-eight times, more times than British Leyland. Each time he struck his victim with a piano. Each time he crept up on his victim from behind. And each time his victim was Henry Crun. Each time in the key of C. Public opinion demanded a public enquiry.

▼ ▼ ▼ ▼ ▼ ▼ ▼ ▼ ▼ ▼ ▼ ▼ ▼ ▼

FX	*Crowd – mumbles – occasional sheep – chickens. Gavel on desk*
JUDGE	Order, please, order. First witness.
BLUEBOTTLE	My name is Captain Bluebottle.
OMNES	Hurray! Hurray!
BLUEBOTTLE	Thank you, friends of Bluebottle. Now for an encore. (*Sings*) 'The girl that I marry will have to be, born some where in Finch – er – ley —'
ORCHESTRA	*Guitar accompaniment*
JUDGE	Silence. Stop that singing, and I'll stop playing this guitar.
BLUEBOTTLE	Fair's fair.
JUDGE	Your evidence?
BLUEBOTTLE	On the night of the attack I was walking down Bongers Lane, when suddenly I stopped.
JUDGE	Why?
BLUEBOTTLE	I must have been tired. My little tootsies were steaming after certain rock and roll dances. (*Sings*) 'One o'clock, two o'clock, 3 o'clock rock . . .'
ORCHESTRA	*Guitar accompaniment*
JUDGE	Stop singing and I'll stop playing!
BLUEBOTTLE	Fair's fair!
JUDGE	And when you stopped, you saw the victim, Mr Crun, was lying in the gutter, yes?

▼ ▼ ▼ ▼ ▼ ▼ ▼ ▼ ▼ ▼ ▼ ▼ ▼ ▼

BLUEBOTTLE When I stopped, I saw the victim, Mr Crun, was —

JUDGE Look, I've said all this!

BLUEBOTTLE Oh, well. Escaping over a wall was a man carrying a wooden-type piano. You didn't say that, did you?

JUDGE Why, as a responsible citizen, didn't you request the man with the piano to stop?

BLUEBOTTLE He wasn't playing it.

JUDGE Next witness.

FIRST CLERK Call William Cobblers.

SECOND CLERK Call William Cobblers.

FX *Footsteps approach*

FIRST CLERK William Cobblers, raise your right leg and say after me: I swear —

COBBLERS I swear.

FIRST CLERK I also drink and smoke . . .

COBBLERS I also drink and smoke.

JUDGE Take the stand. Now, you've come a long way to give evidence.

COBBLERS All the way from Cape Town, mate. The fare cost me every penny I had.

JUDGE We appreciate you making this long journey. Now, on the night of the crime, where were you?

COBBLERS I was in Cape Town.

JUDGE Next witness.

FIRST CLERK Call Minnie Bannister!

SECOND CLERK Call Minnie Bannister.

FAR-OFF VOICE Call Minnie Bannister.

FX *Fast running footsteps*

MINNIE My name is Minnie Bannister, spinster.

JUDGE What is your association with the victim, Mr Crun?

MINNIE The RAC, but we've been barred.

JUDGE Why?

MINNIE We haven't got a car.

JUDGE Are you husband and wife?

MINNIE No, just wife – he does it.

JUDGE Now, what are your occupations?

MINNIE Henry collects foreign stamps, and I knock my knees together.

JUDGE Aren't you ashamed of yourselves?

MINNIE Only on Bank Holidays.

JUDGE   Miss Bannister, after Mr Crun was first struck by this piano, was there any change in him?

MINNIE   Yes. One pound in shillings.

JUDGE   Anything else?

MINNIE   Yes, his hat was over his eyes.

JUDGE   I take it this was caused by the force of the piano landing on it?

MINNIE   No, it's too big for him.

JUDGE   And after that, did he put anything inside his hat to absorb the shock?

MINNIE   Yes.

JUDGE   What?

MINNIE   His head.

CRUN   I object. I object.

JUDGE   To what do you object, Mr Crun?

CRUN   I object to being struck on the head by a piano.

JUDGE   Objection sustained. I find no reason to continue this enquiry, as the information obtained is of a sketchy nature. We will therefore have to wait until further attacks have taken place.

CRUN   I object to further attacks!

JUDGE   Mr Crun, you want us to find the assailant?

CRUN   Yes.

JUDGE   Then you **must** let the attacks continue. If we don't find him, he might attack you again.

CRUN   Next time, I shall vote Communist, I tell you. (*He fades away, objecting*)

FX   *Series of piano attacks on Mr Crun*

SEAGOON   The attacks continued at the rate of one per week. The weeks occurred at the rate of five per month. Then the piano clubber struck in a new and terrible manner.

CRUN   (*terror*) With the loud pedal down.

FX   *Extra loud piano crash, groans*

CRUN   (*smothered*) Helppp . . . helpp . . .

SEAGOON   England was horrified. The BBC gave out warnings.

WALLACE   The police are appealing to the public to help track down the dreaded piano clubber. If you are hit by a piano, please don't hush it up. Tell a policeman. Make sure you are never on the streets alone. It is known that he never makes his attacks **inside** a building. So if, like myself, you work indoors, you are –

FX   *He is struck by a piano*

SEAGOON   The piano clubber had struck **inside** the BBC. We decided to trap him using Ray Ellington.

QUARTET   *Music*

FX   *Piano crashes on Ray Ellington*

▼ ▼ ▼ ▼ ▼ ▼ ▼ ▼ ▼ ▼ ▼ ▼ ▼

The dreaded piano clubber? No, Ray Ellington

SEAGOON   Yes, the dreaded piano clubber had gone racist! Under pressure, Parliament was assembled to pass new laws.

FX   *Crowd – mumbles, odd chicken*

FIRST MP   Under the circumstances, the piano has become a lethal weapon – it will have to be licensed.

SECOND MP   Yes, yes. Anyone caught with a piano on their person without a licence should be prosecuted.

VOICE   Keep them on a lead!

▼ ▼ ▼ ▼ ▼ ▼ ▼ ▼ ▼ ▼ ▼ ▼   101

FIRST MP The honourable member's suggesting that people arriving at Heathrow will have to declare their pianos?

VOICE What about Bechsteins?

SECOND MP Yes, he'll have to declare his as well!

OLD MAN It's a lot of rubbish!

OLDER MAN What is?

OLD MAN Wandsworth Municipal tip.

ALMOST DEAD MAN What's this got to do with pianos?

OLD MAN Absolutely nothing

ALMOST DEAD MAN I see.

WALLACE That night, Churchill addressed Parliament.

FX *Murmurs*

CHURCHILL Anybody who is struck down by this dreaded piano clubber must be blind. A full sized piano – I ask you . . . Isn't it possible to see a man coming towards you with a . . .

FX *Piano crash*

CHURCHILL (*groans*) Never has so much fallen on so few –

FX *Uproar – police sirens – police whistles*

CHURCHILL (*very dramatic*) Get me out – save the leader of England!

▼ ▼ ▼ ▼ ▼ ▼ ▼ ▼ ▼ ▼ ▼ ▼ ▼

POLICEMAN Easy sir, over-acting doesn't help. Can I have your autograph? It's not for me, it's for my little daughter, Clem Atlee.

SEAGOON This is terrible –

ECCLES Yer – but I didn't write it!

SEAGOON Even in Parliament the dreaded piano clubber has struck.

WALLACE Then suddenly in December without warning, suddenly the violent attacks suddenly violently ceased. Suddenly, eh?

CONSTABLE I think, Inspector, he's having the instrument retuned.

WALLACE The police swooped on every piano tuner in London.

SEAGOON Ah, here's another piano tuner in London, Mr Crun.

CRUN I wonder if we shall have any luck this time.

FX *Shop door opening, tinkling shop bell*

SEAGOON Nobody about in the shop. Is there anyone in?

CRUN Yes, me.

SEAGOON Who are you?

CRUN Mr Crun, the famous victim. I came in with you for protection.

SEAGOON So, there's only you and me.

CRUN In any case, whoever works in this dreadful filthy piano shop must be right off his head.

▼ ▼ ▼ ▼ ▼ ▼ ▼ ▼ ▼ ▼ ▼ ▼ ▼

ECCLES   Hello, good evening. You want to buy a piano?

FX   *A few plink plonks on piano*

SEAGOON   I'm looking for a criminal.

ECCLES   Oh, that's one make I haven't got.

SEAGOON   Don't be silly, I wouldn't trust buying a piano in this dump.

ECCLES   Dump! This house a dump! Famous men come here. Do you know who comes here?

SEAGOON   No.

ECCLES   Monsieur Splonson de Groyne.

SEAGOON   Is he famous?

ECCLES   No, but he comes here.

SEAGOON   Look, I'm from the Yard.

ECCLES   Oh, dat your bin outside?

SEAGOON   I'm looking for a person who has been using a piano with force.

ECCLES   Ah, Liberace!

SEAGOON   I must warn you that this is a case of ipso facto carborundum dominus vobiscum!

ECCLES   What do all them words mean?

▼ ▼ ▼ ▼ ▼ ▼ ▼ ▼ ▼ ▼ ▼ ▼ ▼ ▼

SEAGOON	I don't know, but they make me sound intelligent. They fooled you.
ECCLES	Any words fool me.
SEAGOON	Cat? Dog?
ECCLES	Yer!
SEAGOON	Ah well, this makes my job easier. Cat – dog – you say this is a piano shop?
ECCLES	OK, this is a piano shop.
SEAGOON	Cat – dog – explain that notice in your window. The one that says 'For Sale – African elephants, house-trained.'
ECCLES	I don't stock anything like that, I never have.

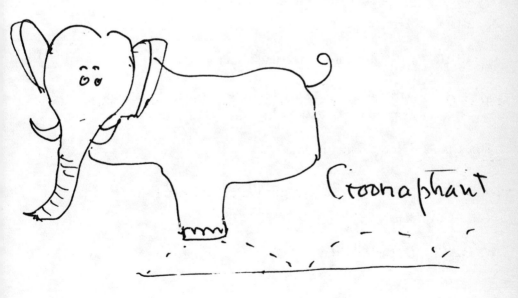

Croonaphant

105

SEAGOON	Supposing people saw that, came in here and asked for an elephant.
ECCLES	Well, I'd just say, I'm sorry sir, I haven't got one.
SEAGOON	But that's mad.
ECCLES	I know, but civility costs nothing.
SEAGOON	Cat – dog – do you mind if we inspect your pianos?
ECCLES	Go ahead, it shouldn't take long.
SEAGOON	Why not?
ECCLES	I haven't got any. Ha ha ha ha. Oh, ha ha ha ha ha. Oh –
SEAGOON	Hee! Hee! Good boy –
CRUN	He's lying! That piano – that's the one! That's the very one that struck me down.
SEAGOON	Are you positive?
CRUN	Yes. The dent in the back fits me perfectly.
SEAGOON	Then we've got him. I'll have a constant watch kept on that dent. As soon as he calls to collect it, it's curtains.
ECCLES	I don't sell curtains –
SEAGOON	Shut up! Silence for this music link . . .
ORCHESTRA	*Musical link*
WALLACE	So they waited. One day, two, three, a week, two weeks,

a fortnight, a month, two months, a year, two years, three, ten, twenty, thirty, forty –

OMNES   *(sing)* Fifty years ago . . .

SEAGOON   Then one midnight as we watched, a night-shirted figure in hair net and curlers ran out of the piano shop.

ECCLES   Help, aaagh, help! Helpp!

SEAGOON   Steady, cat – dog – take it easy. Settle down, boy. What's happened?

ECCLES   The piano clubber's piano. It's gone. It was stolen while I was asleep.

SEAGOON   Are you sure?

ECCLES   Of course I'm sure, I was sleeping on it.

SEAGOON   What key were you sleeping in?

ECCLES   A flat.

SEAGOON   He can't be far away – the show only lasts another few minutes. Sergeant?

SERGEANT   Here, sir.

SEAGOON   I want you to head the dreaded piano clubber off. Have you got your whistle?

SERGEANT   Yes.

SEAGOON   Right. If he hits you with his piano, give a loud blast then blow your whistle.

▼ ▼ ▼ ▼ ▼ ▼ ▼ ▼ ▼ ▼ ▼ ▼ ▼ ▼ ▼

SERGEANT Supposing I get killed?

SEAGOON Then give three blasts and lay in the direction of down. Is that clear?

FX *Piano clubber's signature tune*

SEAGOON Did you hear that? The piano clubber's signature tune! It came from down that street.

FX *Footsteps running backwards and forwards, over which announcer explains:*

WALLACE While our heroes are seeking out the piano clubber, I'd like to tell you the current BBC news. The Deputy Light Controller of Overseas Home Service Programmes has become engaged to Ethel Croll. This has caused quite a stir, as Ethel Croll is married to Fred Ponk, Outside Broadcast Engineer. It promises to be quite an interesting battle of wits. I think that these snippets of news show that the Corporation is not without its thrills. We return now to the piano clubber thing . . .

SEAGOON There he is – in that alley.

SERGEANT I'll get him when he plays again.

FX *Piano. Gunshots. Scream. Running footsteps*

SERGEANT Got him!

SEAGOON After him! Follow the trail of blood-stained notes.

GRAMS *Old fashioned silent film chase music*

WALLACE The trail led them to a lonely Scots crofter's cottage in the Hilton Hotel.

▼ ▼ ▼ ▼ ▼ ▼ ▼ ▼ ▼ ▼ ▼ ▼ ▼

CRUN	I tell you, I don't like the look of it.
SEAGOON	Then don't look at it.
CRUN	At my age you have to look at it just to make sure it's there.
FX	*Thud*
ECCLES	Oooh! Somebody threw a stone on my head, and it hit me, **right** on the head.
FX	*Paper rustling*
SEAGOON	There's a piece of paper wrapped round it.
CRUN	What's he got a piece of paper wrapped round his head for?
SEAGOON	The **stone,** you idiot!
CRUN	It's got writing on it.
SEAGOON	What does it say?
CRUN	Sorry, Eccles, I meant to hit Seagoon.
SEAGOON	Signed, the Dreaded Piano Clubber. It came from that top window.
MORIARTY	(*distant*) You'll never take me alive!
SEAGOON	Gad, it's Count Moriarty. Come down, Moriarty! I'll blow this whistle!
MORIARTY	Ah, not that, not the whistle – shall I come down with my hands up or come up with my hands down?

▼ ▼ ▼ ▼ ▼ ▼ ▼ ▼ ▼ ▼ ▼ ▼ ▼

SEAGOON Yes! Eccles, keep him covered.

ECCLES I'll get a blanket.

MORIARTY Don't shoot, I've only one change of underwear. I'm allergic to death!

SEAGOON Sergeant, put the handcuffs on.

SERGEANT Don't you think they'd look better on him?

SEAGOON Oh alright! Now, Moriarty! Swallow these handcuffs and confess.

MORIARTY (*gulp*) I confess –

SEAGOON Go on.

MORIARTY I confess – I've just swallowed some handcuffs!

GRYTPYPE Let **me** do the talking, Moriarty. I have the teeth.

SEAGOON Exactly who are you?

GRYTPYPE I'm exactly Hercules Grytpype-Thynne.

SEAGOON How do you spell that?

GRYTPYPE T-H-A-T. I'm his solicitor.

MORIARTY Yes – he's been soliciting all night.

GRYTPYPE I'm advising my client to confess and pay me five pounds.

MORIARTY I confess. I am not the piano clubber!

SEAGOON   What? Sergeant, take me away and lock me up with these sound effects!

FX   *Key – chains – iron door slams*

SEAGOON   At last I'm safe from the piano clubber – under lock and key. Ha ha ha!

FX   *Piano crashes on Seagoon*

SEAGOON   *(muffled)* Let me out!

WALLACE   Pretty obvious, wasn't it!

(Pause)

ECCLES   Dog – cat – I'll master dem one day . . .

TWO ROYAL PAGES

The Goons and Prince Charles at Peter Sellers'
home in Elstead, Surrey, in May 1968

Prince Charles being shown how to hold Britt Ekland

Spike Milligan

The Goons and Prince Charles pointing to the British Empire

Spike Milligan

Jack Oakley

THE SIEGE OF FORT KNIGHT

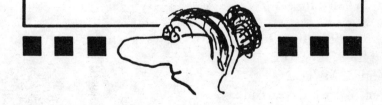

The Goon Show: 'Vintage Goons', No. 13 (a.k.a. 'The Siege of Fort Night')
Recorded 16th March, 1958
First Transmission 27th December, 1986 (Radio 4)

Cast (main characters)

Spike Milligan
  Mate
  Minnie Bannister
  Chief of Biguns Tribe
  Eccles

Peter Sellers
  Army Officer
  Henry Crun
  Major Bloodnok
  Butler
  Bluebottle

Harry Secombe
  Major Seagoon
  A Welshman

Ray Ellington
  African Customs Officer

With The Ray Ellington Quartet, Max Geldray, and the Orchestra
conducted by Wally Stott.
Script by Spike Milligan.
Announcer Wallace Greenslade.
Producer Charles Chilton.

An underwater military gas stove is all that stands between Fort Knight and annihilation at the hands of the Biguns tribe. But – can Inventor Crun construct one in time? (He can't get the wood, you know.) Can Major Seagoon get it to the fort on time? The journey is fraught with impossibilities . . . Thus unfolds this gripping saga of a Long March – long by anyone's calendar . . .

WALLACE	For the last time this evening at popular prices, the unpopular face of capitalism – The Goon Show.
ORCHESTRA	*Corny chords*
SEAGOON	Presenting the Siege of Fort Knight.
WALLACE	The scene – a lonely British outpost in a lonely British outpost.
ARMY OFFICER	Gentlemen, as you see on this map, thirty thousand miles away deep in the liver of Africa –
SEAGOON	You mean the heart, sir.
ARMY OFFICER	No! This place is much further down. In the depths of the jungle and despair, the gallant British garrison at Fort Knight are hard pressed by Biguns natives –
SEAGOON	Biguns?
ARMY OFFICER	Yes, some have very big 'uns. Unless this garrison is relieved within **fourteen days,** Fort Knight is finished, and I feel a terrible pun coming.

SEAGOON Can't they hold out for an extra week?

ARMY OFFICER Rubbish. Who's heard of a fortnight lasting three weeks?

MATE I have – it was in Scunthorpe

ARMY OFFICER Fort Knight needs relief.

SEAGOON Reinforcements?

ARMY OFFICER No, no, they have all the men they require.

SEAGOON Ammunition?

ARMY OFFICER They've plenty!

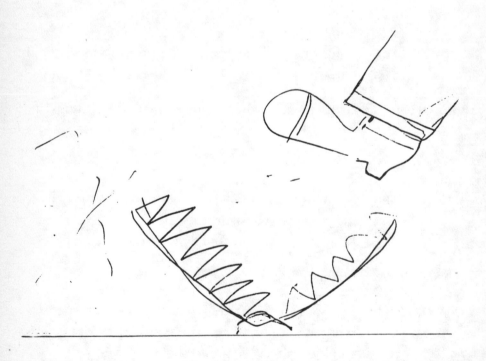

SEAGOON   Provisions?

ARMY OFFICER   They've got ample.

SEAGOON   They can't live on ample alone.

ARMY OFFICER   Worse – they've nothing to cook it on.

SEAGOON   Uncooked ample – you know what that means.

MATE   The squits!

SEAGOON   Yes. In a matter of days they'll be struck – no laundry will go near them.

ARMY OFFICER   And in forty-eight hours the monsoon will arrive.

SEAGOON   Bang in the middle of the rainy season.

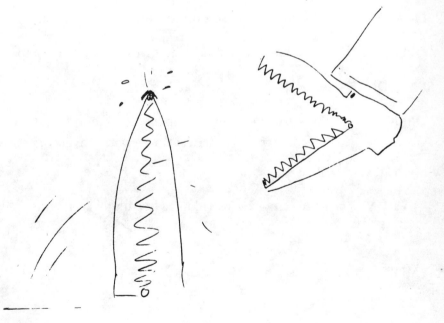

ARMY OFFICER   The point is, when it does break –

SEAGOON   Yes, yes, yes, yes, yes, yes?

ARMY OFFICER   I wish you wouldn't do that! When it breaks, the river Dongler will rise and the fort will be under nine feet of – er – what do you call it –

MATE   Water.

SEAGOON   Gad. What's the answer?

ARMY OFFICER   They'll need underwater gas stoves.

SEAGOON   No such thing's been invented.

ARMY OFFICER   Ah, that's only because nobody has made one. But there is one man.

SEAGOON   One? Come on, there's quite a few of us. Ha! Ha!

ARMY OFFICER   I mean, I know one man who **might** be able to help.

SEAGOON   Not – not – not Dick Scratcher?

ARMY OFFICER   You're dead right – it's not Dick Scratcher. It's Henry Crun – the world's greatest underwater inventor.

ORCHESTRA   *Woeful music*

CRUN   (*sings*) Around the world in eighty-three days, I travelled –

FX   *Knock at door*

MINNIE   I recognise that – it's a knock.

FX   *Knocking*

CRUN   Come in.

SEAGOON   Good evening.

MINNIE   Evening.

FX   *Door opens and shuts*

CRUN   I see you beat the door to it. Good evening.

OMNES   Evening, evening, evening.

          (*Pause*)

SEAGOON   Good evening.

OMNES   Good evening, evening, evening.

CRUN   Are you the elephant man?

SEAGOON   Elephant man? What are you on about?

CRUN   I'm on about £12 a week.

SEAGOON   Listen, I'm from the War Office.

CRUN   War? No thank you, we've just had one!

SEAGOON   I'm here on a mission. –

FX   *Tambourine & tuba accompaniment*

CRUN and MINNIE   (*sing*) Come and join us, come and join us . . .

SEAGOON   Wrong – wrong – wrong mission! Mr Crun –

CRUN   Yes.

SEAGOON	Can you invent a waterproof military gas stove for cooking ample?
CRUN	A waterproof gas stove? It's going to be very difficult. You see, you can't get the wood, you know. Can't get it.
SEAGOON	Have you ever built such a thing before?
CRUN	Well, in a manner of speaking – **no.** You can't get the wood, you see.
SEAGOON	Is there no way?
CRUN	Yes, definitely, definitely, there is! But it will be difficult.
SEAGOON	Why?
CRUN	Because you can't get the wood.
SEAGOON	I can get you the wood.
CRUN	Ah well, that's going to be very difficult.
SEAGOON	Why?
CRUN	I won't be able to go around saying 'You can't get the wood' anymore.
FX	*Strange unearthly metallic sound*
SEAGOON	Gracious, what's that?
CRUN	That's Min playing a gas stove.
SEAGOON	Ah! How long would it take you to waterproof one?
CRUN	Well, that depends on how much you'd be willing to pay.

SEAGOON   Thirty thousand pounds!

FX   *Construction noise at colossal high speed, running footsteps, shouts and yells*

CRUN   (*exhausted*) Where's the money?

SEAGOON   It is **waterproof?**

CRUN   We'll soon find out. Min –

MINNIE   What is it, ducky?

CRUN   Min, just get into the gas oven, would you.

FX   *Door closes*

MINNIE   (*echo*) What have you put all these potatoes in with me for, Henry?

CRUN   Just in case, Min.

MINNIE   (*echo*) In case of what, Henry?

CRUN   Yes, in case of what. Mr Seagoon, help me throw this into the river.

FX   *Splash. Bubbles*

CRUN   Min!

MINNIE   (*echo*) Yes, Henry?

CRUN   Are the potatoes still dry?

MINNIE   (*echo*) Yes, Henry.

CRUN   Hooray, it's working.

MINNIE   That's more than British Leyland.

SEAGOON   Brilliant, Mr Crun. I'll order one right away.

CRUN   How many ones?

SEAGOON   One one.

CRUN   One one? Oh dear, it's a lot of work making one one. Couldn't you order **one** one **one** one **one**?

SEAGOON   Alright – one, one one one one.

CRUN   I just remembered –

SEAGOON   What?

CRUN   You can't get the wood, you see.

SEAGOON   Very well, I'll take the one you just made.

MINNIE   (*off*) Helppp!

CRUN   Too late, it's drifting away down the stream.

■ ■ ■ ■ ■ ■ ■ ■ ■ ■ ■ ■

SEAGOON	Quick – follow that gas stove –
FX	*Splash as body enters water*
MINNIE	(*distant*) Help! Help! Save me and the potatoes!
SEAGOON	(*swimming*) Hold on, Madam . . . (*fade*)
MAX AND ORCHESTRA	*Music*
WALLACE	While Secombe rescued the prototype – Min and the potatoes – Henry Crun struggled manfully with making a second waterproof gas stove. Within a month Captain Seagoon and his gas stoves arrived at the base camp in Africa to arrange transport with a military band.
GRAMS	*Military brass band music*
BLOODNOK	Ah Seagoon, bad news – I've got a temperature, but I'm going to carry on.
SEAGOON	What is your temperature?
BLOODNOK	98.4.
SEAGOON	That's normal.
BLOODNOK	I know, that's why I'm carrying on.
SEAGOON	Good. Now, how are we to get the waterproof gas stoves from here to the garrison? Helicopter?
BLOODNOK	Impossible, sir, impossible. The fort is invisible from the air. And worse still – the air is invisible from the fort.
SEAGOON	By road, then?

BLOODNOK   No road.

SEAGOON   The river?

BLOODNOK   No.

SEAGOON   Down the river?

BLOODNOK   No.

SEAGOON   Across the river into the trees?

BLOODNOK   No.

SEAGOON   Why not?

BLOODNOK   No trees.

SEAGOON   Across the trees into the river?

BLOODNOK   No river.

SEAGOON   Rail?

BLOODNOK   Doesn't run.

SEAGOON   Why not?

BLOODNOK   No railway.

SEAGOON   Could we build one?

BLOODNOK   The river would wash it away.

SEAGOON   You said there was no river.

BLOODNOK   It's behind the trees.

Goon bird

SEAGOON   A moment ago you said there weren't any trees.

BLOODNOK   Ah, they've grown since then. Time can't stand still for you, you know.

SEAGOON   Wait! I remember seeing an armoured train at the depot.

BLOODNOK   That train was only armoured from the inside.

SEAGOON   Why?

BLOODNOK   We couldn't fire out, but they could fire in.

SEAGOON   Why was that?

BLOODNOK   The windows faced inwards.

SEAGOON   Then we'll use that!

FX   *Guard's train whistle. Engine hooter – train puffs out of station*

BLOODNOK   Now, to keep the engine driver alert I've brought me bagpipes –

FX   *Bagpipes drone into life*

SEAGOON   Why didn't we think of that before? Meanwhile, at Fort Knight –

(From now on very fast)

FX   *Gunfire, bugles*

SPIKE   Meanwhile, Mr Crun –

CRUN   You can't get the wood, you know.

SEAGOON   Yes! yes! Meanwhile, back in Fort Knight –

FX   *Gunfire, bugles*

SEAGOON   On the armoured train –

FX   *Train and bagpipes*

BLOODNOK   We shall have to use electrified Mongolian bagpipes.

SEAGOON   Why didn't we think of that before? Meanwhile, at Fort Knight –

FX	Gunfire, bugles
SPIKE	While back with Crun –
CRUN	. . . the wood, you know.
SEAGOON	. . . Fort Knight –
FX	*Gunfire, bugles*
SPIKE	At this very moment in London's West End –
GRAMS	*Victor Sylvester's 'Come Dancing' music*
SEAGOON	On the armoured train –
FX	*Train – bagpipes*
SPIKE	Meantime in Chapter Two!
FX	*Phone rings*
BLOODNOK	Hello? Armoured train.
FX	*Tom-toms*
NATIVE	(*distorted*) Listen, Bloodnok. This Chief of Biguns Tribe. I give you warning. If you proceed with waterproof gas stove at Fort Knight, we poison the drinking water ... Ha! ha! he! he!
BLOODNOK	You over-acting swine!
SEAGOON	Keep him on the line.
FX	*Whoosh*

BLOODNOK	Right. Listen, you devil –
NATIVE	(*distorted*) I kill everything in your body, I put spear –
FX	*Pistol shot*
NATIVE	Argghhh!
SEAGOON	(*on phone*) Bloodnok?
BLOODNOK	Yes.
SEAGOON	I've got him!

BLOODNOK Splendid. Now get back here right away. Crun's just arrived with an improved waterproof gas stove Mark II.

ORCHESTRA *Dramatic chords*

WALLACE Hurrying overland, Crun reached base camp disguised as a bale of tobacco.

SEAGOON Crun, you've arrived in the nicotine!

FX *Tearing paper wrapper*

CRUN Look – voilà!

SEAGOON   That's not a voilà! That's the stove.

CRUN   Yes. I'll just get in and turn on the gas and set the regulo at 3.

FX   *Switch*

GRAMS   *Organ music: Reginald Dixon's 'I do like to be beside the seaside'*

CRUN   (*echo*) Dear, dear, that's not right. I'll try regulo 2. I'll just have a look inside the oven . . .

FX   *Door opens*

GRAMS   *Railway station noises*

TANNOY   The train now standing at Platform 3 . . .

WELSHMAN   Pardon me, but where's the taxi rank?

CRUN   I'm sorry, I'm a stranger round here.

WELSHMAN   Oh! Where do you come from?

CRUN   Africa.

WELSHMAN   Oh. Would you mind closing the oven door, there's a draught in the waiting-room.

FX   *Door closing*

CRUN   Amazing. Let me see. I think I can see what the trouble is. I had the regulo on 5. It should have been on 2. Now let's see what we get.

QUARTET   *Music*

CRUN	No, there's still something wrong!
SEAGOON	Crun! We can't waste time like this!
CRUN	You know a better way?
SEAGOON	Yes – here it comes. We **must** get to the fort. There's very little time left or right! Bloodnok!
BLOODNOK	He must mean me!
SEAGOON	We must set off immediately.
BLOODNOK	You're dead right. We must do it today, or we'll never get another chance. Eccles, help me get these gas stoves on your head.
ECCLES	Plenty of room. OK. How far do I have to carry them?
BLOODNOK	A thousand miles.
ECCLES	I got to walk all the way?
BLOODNOK	No. Part of the way you'll be allowed to run.
ECCLES	You bastard! (*Censored*)
SEAGOON	Bloodnok, we have to keep this expedition a closely-guarded secret.
BLOODNOK	Don't worry. The camels are all disguised as men.
SEAGOON	And the men?
BLOODNOK	Heavily disguised as camels.

SEAGOON   Were you trained at MI5?

BLOODNOK   As a dustman!

SEAGOON   What a disguise.

ORCHESTRA   *Safari music – dramatic chords*

SEAGOON   Thus began a remarkable march of forty-seven days. Forty-seven days **is** remarkable for the month of March.

BLOODNOK   To conserve energy we marched lying down and only stood up to sleep.

SEAGOON   Meanwhile, at Fort Knight

   (Silence) —

ECCLES   Early closing!

FX   *African drums*

BLOODNOK   That night amid the sound of jungle drums, we were confronted by the Biguns natives, some in warpaint, some more civilized in wallpaper. As we neared the Fort we became familiar with African customs.

AFRICAN   Anything to declare, white man?

BLOODNOK   A waterproof gas stove.

AFRICAN   Ymblum naba blum. Importation of gas stove you pay three elephant tusks.

BLOODNOK   Where do you expect me, from Catford SE6, to get elephant tusks?

AFRICAN   I sell you.

BLOODNOK   How much?

AFRICAN   One waterproof gas stove.

BLOODNOK   What luck! Eccles, give him one of the waterproof gas stoves.

AFRICAN   Here – tusks.

     FX   *Crashing of tusks*

Jack Oakley

ECCLES   Oh. Now he's got a waterproof gas stove.

BLOODNOK   What luck. **Just** what we need. I say, tribal fellow, how much you want for waterproof gas stove?

AFRICAN   Three elephant tusks.

BLOODNOK   Three? Just what we've got –

SEAGOON   News from Fort Knight! They've only enough uncooked ample for another hour.

BLOODNOK   Well, it's only eighteen miles as the crow flies, but our crow is sick with lurgi.

SEAGOON   Eighteen miles, through native tribes. It means certain death or certain life.

BLOODNOK   Yes. One of us must volunteer.

SEAGOON   Yes, one of us must volunteer.

ECCLES   One of us **must** volunteer.

BLOODNOK   Good old Eccles.

ECCLES   No. Bad old Eccles.

SEAGOON   Brave boy, Eccles.

ECCLES   No, coward Eccles.

SEAGOON   You coward.

ECCLES   I'm a coward.

BLOODNOK   You coward.

ECCLES   You coward.

SEAGOON   You coward.

BLOODNOK   Well it's no good **three** cowards going.

SEAGOON   (*calls*) Mr Crun! Mr Crun, we have one hour in which to cover eighteen miles to the fort. Any suggestions?

CRUN   Well, we could go by train. That's regulo 5.

FX   Switch

SEAGOON   Good. Open the oven door!

FX   Door opens. Sound of trains

TANNOY   Train now standing at Platform 7 of the gas stove, is for Fort Knight.

CRUN   (*echo*) Just in time. Everybody into the gas stove. I'll get in first. Come on. Hand me in the right side of the stove. Now the left. Now the top and the back. Now close the oven door from the outside and bring it in after you.

ECCLES   Wait a minute. Close it on the outside? And bring it in after me? That would mean climbing through it when it's shut and not opening it till I get through.

SEAGOON   Well? What are you waiting for?

ECCLES   I don't know how to do it.

SEAGOON	We'll take the rest of the oven by train. **You** get the oven door and go ahead on foot. Is that all clear?
ECCLES	Er –
SEAGOON	Good. Swallow this road map and follow the instructions.
ORCHESTRA	*Dramatic chords*
SEAGOON	Within an hour we were at the gates of Fort Knight.
FX	*Gunfire, bugles. Native warriors*
CRUN	I'll ring.
FX	*Doorbell*
SEAGOON	I'll do the talking. I've got an 11-plus, you just look intelligent.
ECCLES	Oh dear.
FX	*Door opens*
BUTLER	Was that **you** ringing, sir?
SEAGOON	No, it was the bell. We'd like to speak to the commanding officer.
BUTLER	I'll see if he's in, sir.
FX	*Door closes*
SEAGOON	He was a nice fellow – I wonder why he was nude.
FX	*Door opens*

BUTLER   Pardon me, sir, they're rather busy at the moment. If you could leave your card?

SEAGOON   My card? It's in my other suit.

BUTLER   Perhaps you'd like to stay to tea, sir.

SEAGOON   Oh, that is kind.

BUTLER   You must excuse the confusion, we have the enemies of the Queen here.

SEAGOON   Oh, are they stopping here as well?

BUTLER   Yes. It's all very confusing at mealtimes. Is yours the waterproof gas stove we're expecting?

SEAGOON   Yes. Could we connect it to the mains?

BUTLER   I'm afraid that would serve no purpose.

SEAGOON   What do you mean?

BUTLER   The gas was cut off yesterday. A matter of a quarter in arrears.

SEAGOON   Never mind. We mustn't fail now. Eccles, open that brown paper parcel.

ECCLES   (*sings as opens parcel*) Oh! It's you!

BLUEBOTTLE   Yes, I've seen the light, Captain. I'm the rescue plan. Hello, everybody. I heard you call.

SEAGOON   I haven't called yet.

BLUEBOTTLE   I'm answering in advance. Strikes answering-in-advance pose, well forward on balls of feet.

SEAGOON   Get into the gas stove and connect this cylinder of gas.

BLUEBOTTLE   Yes, I will, Captain. I will do that. Enters gas stove, and assumes crouching position within, as assumed by certain people in *Bridge over the River Kwai,* playing South London all next week. Fixes gas cylinder. Here, I smell gas.

SEAGOON   Can you see where the leak is?

BLUEBOTTLE   No, it's very dark in here.

SEAGOON   Well, strike a match.

BLUEBOTTLE   All right, Captain. Oh, wait a minute. Are you sure this match will not ignite the gas, thereby deading me, as it has on many previous occasions?

WALLACE   Listeners, stand by for the obvious.

SEAGOON   Of course not. They're safety matches.

BLUEBOTTLE   Thank you for your words of comfort, Captain. I trust you with my life. I do do that, yes. I will strike a match now. Strikes safety match for safety.

     FX   *Strikes match*

BLUEBOTTLE   Ah-hah! You're waiting for me to get deaded, aren't you? But I'm not going to. This week Bluebottle is not going to be deaded. So there.

FX	*Explosion, followed by knock on door. Door opens*
POSTMAN	Brown paper parcel for you, sir.
ECCLES	Thank you.
FX	*Paper being torn off parcel*
ECCLES	Oh – it's you!
BLUEBOTTLE	You rotten swine, you! Seeks among debris for shattered underpants, shredded boots and three 1″ by 1½″ lumps of head.
SEAGOON	But, lad – you've done it!
BUTLER	Compliments of the besieged garrison, sir, could you make your explosions quieter? We can't hear ourselves fight.
SEAGOON	Don't you realise, below stairs fool, the underwater gas stove has exploded!
BUTLER	Oh dear, and I had the Sunday joint all ready. This will mean surrender to the enemies of the Queen.
SEAGOON	Surrender?
BUTLER	Surrender.
BLOODNOK	Surrender?
SEAGOON	To the enemies of the Queen?
BLOODNOK	A splendid idea, I'll put my coward set on!

SEAGOON   No! Go in there and fight. Give out the swords. Open that gate and we'll charge.

FX   *Door opens*

SEAGOON   Charge! Wait! There's nobody here.

BLOODNOK   They've all gone.

ECCLES   There's not a soul.

SEAGOON   What a disappointing ending to a show.

WALLACE   Perhaps listeners will now believe how bad things really are in the Old Country. Good night.

BBC

The Raspberry Song

The Goons' very last recording, 1979. The 'Raspberry Song' for Decca Records

In a little town where I belong,
There's a most accomplished fellow.
He's the leader of the village choir,
And his voice is warm and mellow.
He drives a fruit cart round the street
And everybody knows it:
He doesn't sing or rave about
His fruit, he simply blows it

XXX XXX XXX XXX XXX - 'raspberry'

He's doing it all day long

XXX XXX XXX XXX XXX

Peter Sellers demonstrating how to hold up a bank, while Milligan holds up a sandwich

The Raspberry Song

In a little town where I belong, There's a most accomplished fellow.

He's the leader of the village choir, And his voice is warm and mellow. He

drives a fruit cart 'round the street And everybody knows it: He

doesn't sing or rave about His fruit, he simply blows it

(Orchestra)   (Raspberry...)   He's doing it all day long

(Raspberry...)   It's better than any song, Though it isn't very pretty You've

got to admit it's cute So, all together, let it go (Raspberry...) Eat more fruit

(Raspberry...)   It's certainly come to stay (Raspberry...)

It's a treat to hear him say, Hey Fruit's in season, plenty there is:

Apples, plums & the old raspberries (Raspberry...) Everything is fresh today

It's better than any song,
Though it isn't very pretty
You've got to admit it's cute
So, all together, let it go

XXX XXX XXX XXX XXX

Eat more fruit

XXX XXX XXX XXX XXX

It's certainly come to stay

XXX XXX XXX XXX XXX

It's a treat to hear him say, Hey
Fruit's in season, plenty there is:
Apples, plums and the old raspberries

XXX XXX XXX XXX XXX

Everything is fresh today.

Sir Harry Secombe reading the word 'laugh' from a piece of paper

Every Friday night when work is done,
He never wastes a minute.
To the village hall he hurries round
Where he sings just like a linnet.
To hear him blow a melody
It's great, you can't deny it;
And if you've nothing else to do
I'd like you all to try it.

XXX XXX XXX XXX XXX

Get ready and do it now.

XXX XXX XXX XXX XXX

It's easy when you know how.
Though it isn't very pretty
You've got to admit it's cute
So, all together, let it go

XXX XXX XXX XXX XXX

Eat more fruit

XXX XXX XXX XXX XXX

It's certainly come to stay

XXX XXX XXX XXX XXX

It's a treat to hear him say, Hey
So Te La So Fa Me Re Doh

It's a treat to hear him say
Fruit's in season, plenty there is:
Apples, plums and the old raspberries

XXX XXX XXX XXX XXX

XXX XXX XXX XXX XXX

Everything is fresh today

Everything is fresh today.

It's certainly come to stay

XXX XXX XXX XXX XXX

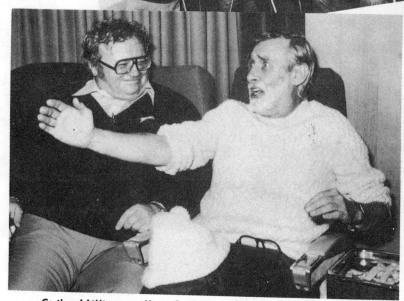

Spike Milligan telling Sir Harry Secombe how big his is

Jack Oakley

▲ ▲ ▲ ▲ ▲ ▲ ▲ ▲ ▲ ▲ ▲ ▲ ▲ ▲ ▲

THE TREE MANIAC

The Tree Maniac.

Announcer: Good evening, the BBC Home Service presents the Grunes (pause) Grunes?. Grunes??? Yes, it's quite definitely written here: G-R-U-N-E-S. Of course, they must mean Coons - yes, that's it - Coons (walks away repeating)

John Snagge- (Peter) Mr Greenslade is currently being treated by Sir Charles Fees the famous Psychiatrist and used car salesman. What Greenslade meant to say was that This is the Grute Show (Pause) Grute?, no L + G they mean - Grune - the Grune Show

[Long Silence]

Oboe Gives turned tuning A to Orchestra

Snagge Bai Jove I do believe they weren't quite ready - Have another try Ladies and -

Orchestra Come in too soon with signature tune.
[Pause]

FX Fork falls on floor

This really was a Lost Goon Show – lost, forgotten and never finished. This is its very first public appearance.

ANNOUNCER   Good evening, the BBC Home Service presents the Grunes (*Pause*) Grunes? **Grunes**??? Yes, it's quite definitely written here: G-R-U-N-E-S. Of course, they must mean Coons – yes, that's it – Coons (*walks away repeating*)

JOHN SNAGGE   (**Peter**) Mr Greenslade is currently being treated by Sir Charles Fees, the famous psychiatrist and used car salesman. What Greenslade meant to say was that this is the **Grute** Show. (*Pause*) Grute? No, ladies and gentlemen, they mean Grune – the Grune Show. (*Long silence*)

OBOE   *Gives hurried tuning A to Orchestra*

SNAGGE   Bai Jove, I do believe they weren't quite ready. Have another try: ladies and –

ORCHESTRA   *Come in too soon with signature tune*

(*Pause*)

FX   *Fork falls on floor*

NED SEAGOON   That thrilling sound of an EPNS fork hitting the ground signals the start of a mysterious mystery.

SPIKE (*starter*) On your marks – get set –

FX *Starter's pistol, followed by mass of boots running away*

NED Very well, I do it on my own – ladies and gentlemen, The Landing Tree Maniac.

ORCHESTRA *Brooding-mystery chords mixed with maniacal laughter and tree chopping*

DIMBLEBY (**Peter**) The Queen places the Royal sapling in the Royal hole and with a silver shovel fills it in.

THE QUEEN (**Peter**) I name this tree Copper Beech. God bless its nuts, and all who will assail her.

FX *Feeble clapping*

ANNOUNCER Meantime – at Catford police station a Constable Oaf is at work beating a rubber bust of Cliff Richard.

FX *Truncheon on head*

CONSTABLE (**Spike** – Cockney) Take that, you hippy swine.

FX *Truncheon wallop*

CONSTABLE Earnin' orl that money.

FX *Wallop*

CONSTABLE Singing crappy tunes!

FX *Wallop*

CONSTABLE And me with my fine voice on only 18 quid a week.

FX *Wallop. Phone rings*

▲ ▲ ▲ ▲ ▲ ▲ ▲ ▲ ▲ ▲ ▲ ▲ ▲ ▲

CONSTABLE   Hello – Hello – better pick it up, but first –

      FX   *Wallop. Picks phone up*

CONSTABLE   Catford Police Station.

      NEDDY   Hello, this is Neddy Seagoon, Welsh midget and
Forester-in-waiting to the Queen!

CONSTABLE   Oh, you ever seen that swine Cliff Richard – he gets
£2,000,000 a minute.

      FX   *Wallop*

      NEDDY   Yes – I want to report –

ANNOUNCER The BBC would like to point that what you are hearing is not typical of the police force. The Inspector has said he personally is not jealous of Cliff Richard – it's that bastard Elvis Presley –

NEDDY It's true – the £18-a-week police were not interested, folks – so I would have to go to the £10 a week police, even 9 or 8! Nine and eight make £17, that would be only a pound cheaper than the £18 a week, understand? (*Gibbers on*)

ANNOUNCER Mr Seagoon is also being treated by Sir Charles Fees.

NEDDY So money is no object – I'll just throw this shilling on the pavement to see if there's any Scotsmen in the district.

FX *Shilling on pavement followed by approach of two sets of boot at speed. They halt*

GRYTPYPE-THYNNE (*breathless*) M'card!

NEDDY MacHard – ah – a real Scot! See, Thynne & Moriarty, financiers and 24-hour dry cleaners.

CONSTABLE And me only £18 a week –

FX *Wallop*

NEDDY Listen, constabule of old Catford, I wish to report a tree vandal –

CONSTABLE Oh – is it a doggie?

NEDDY Is what a doggie?

CONSTABLE   (*barks*) Bow-wow-wow-woof-grrr-

NEDDY   What's that?

CONSTABLE   That's a doggie!

NEDDY   I thought you were a policeman.

CONSTABLE   I am, and it's only £18 a week.

FX   *Wallop*

NEDDY   Look, you know Herne's Mighty Oak in Windsor Park?

CONSTABLE   Well, not personally.

NEDDY   Well, it's –

CONSTABLE   – and he's always havin' it off with good-lookin' birds –

FX   *Wallop*

NEDDY   Look, man! Herne's Mighty Oak has been uprooted – roots and all!

CONSTABLE   – and 'e's not even good lookin'!

FX   *Wallop (continues)*

MORIARTY   Owww!

NEDDY   The sound came from a shivering wreck wearing a wedding-tackle-length vest, a topless bowler – and a reconditioned cricketer's box – lying stretched on the pavement.

▲ ▲ ▲ ▲ ▲ ▲ ▲ ▲ ▲ ▲ ▲ ▲ ▲

THYNNE My partner, Count Jim 'Knackered' Moriarty – a scion of Grade 3 Salmon, has played the lead in several French post-cards.

NEDDY Is he dead?

THYNNE That is a trade secret – but his strength is unbounded – with him we can crack this case open.

NEDDY So saying he cracked a case open –

FX *Case being smashed*

THYNNE That's just a beginning – you want Herne's Mighty Oak traced?

NEDDY Yes yes yes yes yes yes!

THYNNE One yes would have done – you're used to working with the deaf or the Irish? Moriarty, cover me with a song.

MORIARTY (*sings*) These teeth are the teeth of a woman in love. (*Continues*)

THYNNE Neddy – so far, our investigations have led us to this blank cheque – it would help our enquiries if you signed just here.

FX *Hurried signing*

THYNNE What a beautiful hand –

MORIARTY Yes – but a terrible signature.

THYNNE Moriarty, open the Cyprus Sherry.

▲ ▲ ▲ ▲ ▲ ▲ ▲ ▲ ▲ ▲ ▲ ▲ ▲ ▲

FX	*Pop and pouring*
NEDDY	It – it looks like water!
THYNNE	A toast to your forthcoming overdraft.
FX	*Clinking glasses*
NEDDY	It – it **tastes** like water!
THYNNE	Water? There's an old Latin adage: Parventum – ad hoc – nil desperandum – aqua frescha!
NEDDY	Oh – I wish I'd met you earlier.
THYNNE	So do we, Neddy – say so do we for me, Moriarty.
MORIARTY	So do we!
FX	*Terrible slap*
MORIARTY	Ow – mon tête!
NEDDY	Why do you keep hitting him?
THYNNE	Why? Because he's **there**!
ANNOUNCER	Who would want to remove Herne's Oak? The first clue came from a couple living in Neasden.
FX	*Clock ticking – bed springs – snoring. Alarm clock rings.*
CRUN & BANNISTER	(*waking noises*)
CRUN	I'll just look in the mirror . . . Oh. Is it open eyes for awake?
BANNISTER	Well, that's how I do it!

▲ ▲ ▲ ▲ ▲ ▲ ▲ ▲ ▲ ▲ ▲ ▲ ▲ ▲

CRUN Ah!

BANNISTER Ooooo! Are you awake, Henry?

CRUN What's the time?

BANNISTER I set the alarm for three.

CRUN Why? There's only two of us.

BANNISTER There must be *six* more somewhere –

FX *Bong of po*

CRUN Oh –

BANNISTER It's very dark this morning. Look how dark it is out.

CRUN That's the blinds, Min.

FX *Sound of doorknob, and bolts being withdrawn*

CRUN (*off mike*) Oh, Min. There's something on the landing.

BANNISTER It must be the cat.

CRUN No, a cat couldn't do this. Someone's left an oak tree on the landing. Cats can't do oak trees.

BANNISTER Let me see. Oh, there's a label on it – 'From the Tree Maniac'.

CRUN I don't remember ordering a tree from a maniac.

BANNISTER It must be a joke.

CRUN No, Min, it's not a joke. It's definitely a tree. Jokes don't have leaves on.

BANNISTER	No, some jokes have whiskers on.
BOTH	*Talk at cross purposes — fade*
FX	*Heavy snoring*
ANNOUNCER	The snoring you hear is that of the duty fireman at Lewisham.
FX	*Phone rings — snorer wakes up*
FIREMAN	(**Spike**) Hello, Lewisham fire brigade.
CRUN	Hello — we have a tree on our landing.
FIREMAN	Thanks for telling me.
CRUN	Don't go — we want help.
FIREMAN	Well, is the tree on fire?
CRUN	No.
FIREMAN	Well, we can't come unless it's on fire.
CRUN	Min, he says he can't come unless the tree is on fire.
BANNISTER	Oh. I'll get a box of matches.
CRUN	If you come now, we'll have it going by the time you arrive.
FIREMAN	It's very nice of you to put work my way.

(and here it ends)

▲ ▲ ▲ ▲ ▲ ▲ ▲ ▲ ▲ ▲ ▲ ▲ ▲